T0267993

HOW TO PUT LOVE FIRST

SADIE ROBERTSON HUFF & CHRISTIAN HUFF

THOMAS NELSON
Since 1798

How to Put Love First

© 2023 Sadie Robertson Huff and Christian Huff

Published in Nashville, Tennessee, by Thomas Nelson. Thomas Nelson is a registered trademark of HarperCollins Christian Publishing, Inc.

Thomas Nelson titles may be purchased in bulk for educational, business, fund-raising, or sales promotional use. For information, please email SpecialMarkets@ThomasNelson.com.

Printed in the United States of America

23 24 25 26 27 VER 10 9 8 7 6 5 4 3 2

TO OUR PARENTS

Thank y'all for showing us what a committed relationship to the Lord and to each other looks like. The love y'all have for Jesus and each other has changed our lives.

CONTENTS

PART 2: YOUR RELATIONSHIP WITH YOUR PEOPLE

PART 3: YOUR RELATIONSHIP
WITH YOUR COMMUNITY

FOREWORD

"I DIRECT MESSAGED HER ON INSTAGRAM AND TOLD HER I wanted to send her a link to your message on dating. That's how I got her phone number." People have told me all kinds of things about my sermons, but I had never had someone tell me that one of my messages got them out of the DMs and into texting with the girl they liked. No one until Christian Huff.

A decade of ministry among eighteen-to-twenty-five-year-olds had stirred up a great deal of compassion in my heart for young people today as they navigate the increasingly confusing landscape of singleness and dating. So, I preached and eventually wrote out my best attempt at providing biblical principles for young people to use like stars in the sky as they sail the complex waters of life and love.

Christian shared with me that he had not only used my message to get a first date, but they used the scriptural principles I laid out to shape the contours of their dating and early married life. My wife, Donna, and I became fast friends with the Huffs a number of years ago and have had the opportunity to watch their lives up close. Christian and Sadie have done the work to apply God's timeless truths to their real-time relationship, as well as their relationships with family, friends, and so many others, and have flourished because of it. I think it's wonderful they have now decided to share some of the highs and lows of their story with you.

But why are they doing this? They have plenty of other directions to channel their energy. They did not have to fight the "war of art" to craft sentences and create a devotional for you. And they were certainly not obligated to be vulnerable and share the good, the bad, and the ugly parts of their lives and relationships. So why create this devotional you now hold?

The apostle Paul explained to his beloved Thessalonians, "We were ready to share with you not only the gospel of God but also our own selves, because you had become very dear to us" (1 Thessalonians 2:8b). Paul's sincere love for his people led him to not only share God's word but to bare his soul. He was willing to do anything to help them grow and flourish in their faith. And if sharing his life helped them reach their full potential, then he did not hesitate to do it.

Sometimes we need to hear about other people's struggles, so we don't feel so alone in ours. Other times we need to hear about a rhythm, a perspective, a habit, or a conviction in someone else's life that can inspire and equip us to live our best lives. It is a labor of love to share your own story with someone in the hopes that they might glean wisdom without going through the same growing pains.

Donna and I can confidently say we believe the Huffs possess a sincere love for you. And because they care, they have chosen to share both the Scriptures and their lives with you, in the hopes that their story will provide strength and hope to you as you live out your story and put love first in your relationship with God and the people in your life.

So let me encourage you, friend: Emulate their best practices. Learn from their failures. And, most of all, cling to the same gospel of Jesus that has changed their lives for the good. I am cheering you on, as I know they are, every step of the way!

BEN STUART

PASTOR OF PASSION CITY CHURCH DC; AUTHOR OF
SINGLE, DATING, ENGAGED, MARRIED AND *REST & WAR*

A LETTER TO YOU

HEY FRIENDS. CHRISTIAN AND SADIE HERE!

We are so thankful that you have picked up our book and are placing a desire in your heart to put love first. We want you to know that no one is excluded from this message. It's not just for people with a ring on their finger. It is a message for the single, dating, engaged, or married person. This is a message for everyone.

Our culture has put a lot of ideas in front of us about what love is and how it is supposed to look. You typically see that on display on Instagram with the picture of the insanely cute couple, on a rom-com where everything is weirdly perfect, on the endless ads for chocolate and teddy bears on Valentine's Day, and of course on that popular TV show where the woman receives a rose at the rose ceremony. But we are talking about a much different and bigger picture of love in this book. One that is a little bit rawer, but one that is actually real and true.

What is love if it is exclusive to people in certain seasons of life? What is love if it doesn't seek to know the most real parts of you? If love is really just a picture of a perfect but unrealistic romance, then it certainly is not the most powerful thing on the planet. It surely could not be what we are all created for.

Thankfully love is much bigger than that picture. The truth

is that someone could have the full picture that our culture has painted and not know love. They could have the cute post, a rom-com kind of love, all the teddy bears in the world, and they may even have won the bachelor, but have no idea what love really is. First John 4:8 says, "Whoever does not love does not know God, because God is love."

I told y'all, love is lot bigger than you might have thought. *God is love.*

In 1 Corinthians, Paul gives a description of what love is. He said, "Love is patient, love is kind. It does not envy, it does not boast, it is not proud. It does not dishonor others, it is not self-seeking, it is not easily angered, it keeps no record of wrongs. Love does not delight in evil but rejoices with the truth. It always protects, always trust, always hopes, always perseveres. Love never fails" (13:4–8 NIV). Now, that is powerful! But I know what some of you are thinking: *I have never experienced a love like that before.* You cannot even fathom a relationship that looks like that description. But remember, God is love in love's perfection. This description is fully accurate for the love that God is able to give, because this is who He is.

In 1 John 4:19 it says, "We love because He first loved us." Friends, we will learn how to love one another when we begin to learn Who we are first loved by. As we grow in our knowledge of God, we will grow in our capacity for love. The two go hand in hand—as we get to know God, we will get to know love. We will begin to put love first in our lives when we learn to put God first. In this book you will see the messiness in our lives as we have struggled to put love first and the beauty that flows from life when love is in its rightful place. We are going to get really practical here and have even brought in a relationship expert, Dr. Josh Kirby, to help us walk through some of this. Sometimes we need a counselor, a mentor, or a friend to help us navigate through our own struggles to put love first.

The two of us really do love each other, but we love God more. We receive love from one other, but before we ever said the words "I love you," we both deeply knew our value and worth because we already had the ultimate love from God. Knowing that kind of love first has helped us to know how to love each other well. First John 4:12 says, "No one has ever seen God; but if we love one another, God lives in us and his love is made complete in us" (NIV). Let's help each other see God by putting this kind of love first.

SADIE AND CHRISTIAN

PART 1

YOUR RELATIONSHIP
WITH GOD

GOD SEES YOU

Nathanael said to him, "How do you know me?" Jesus answered
him, "Before Philip called you, when you were under the fig
tree, I saw you." Nathanael answered him, "Rabbi, you are
the Son of God! You are the King of Israel!" JOHN 1:48-49

SADIE

IF WE ARE GOING TO TALK ABOUT LOVE, THEN WE FIRST
have to talk about God because God is love. If we are going to put
love first, then that means putting God first. God is big and broad and
powerful. He's also intimate, personal, and near. He created the galaxies,
the universe, the world. But He also numbers the hairs on our heads. He
hovers over the universe, and yet reclines at the table with sinners. He is
over everything and still has time to listen to us. One way I like to talk
to God is through writing songs. I sat down one day with a friend and
wrote words to a song in an attempt to capture a sense of God's greatness
. . . and His smallness. He is both, fully, at once:

> *You're the Lion and the Lamb*
> *Redeemer and a Friend*
> *Every word is yes and amen*
> *You're the promise, 'til the end*

He is both the Redeemer for everyone, and our close and personal
friend. How amazing is that?

Most of us want to be seen doing important things with important
people to prove ourselves to the world, but deep down, don't we all know
that being seen in that way does not actually bring the approval that we
desire? Our souls are searching for so much more. More than a like, a
clap, or a cheer from others. We want to be deeply *known*, to be *seen* for

who we are, and *loved* despite all our mess and inadequacy. And that is the beautiful thing about God. When He sees us, there is no pressure to up our game. There's just heartfelt invitation: *Come as you are.*

In today's passage from John, Jesus spotted Nathanael hanging out under a fig tree. Nathanael's friend Philip had told him about this amazing man from Nazareth who was the Savior their people had been waiting for; however, Nathanael did not believe it. "Can anything good come out of *Nazareth*?" he asked (John 1:46, emphasis added). I'm sure we have had others say similar things about us, or maybe we even feel that way about ourselves. "Can anything good come from my story?"

Jesus didn't let that comment stop Him. Instead, He complimented Nathanael's honesty, which seemed to soften him. From there Nathanael asked Jesus, "How do you know me?" to which Jesus responded, "When you were under the fig tree, I saw you." Jesus saw Nathanael—*really* saw him. Nathanael was so affected by this, his attitude about Jesus completely changed. "Rabbi, you are the Son of God!" he declared (vv. 48–49).

What would make a skeptic go from insulting to praising in a hot minute? Jesus not only *saw* Nathanael under the fig tree, but He *knew* him. On a soul-piercing kind of level. Isn't it amazing that although Jesus could have impressed him with a million different miracles, it was *seeing* him that changed him?

ΗΟШ ΤΟ PUT **LOVE** FIRST

It is a powerful thing to realize that God sees you and knows you. Make sure that you take the time to see someone today. Here is an example from my life: Recently I asked the clerk at the grocery store how long she had been working there. She said twenty years. When the machine asked me if I wanted cash back, I clicked Yes and gave the cash to the woman. I said, "This is a thank-you for twenty years of hard work." She immediately began to cry. Seeing people changes people.

DAY 2
GOD KNOWS YOU

For one will scarcely die for a righteous person—though perhaps for a good person one would dare even to die—but God shows his love for us in that while we were still sinners, Christ died for us. ROMANS 5:7-8

SADIE

MANY MENTORS HAVE WARNED ME THAT LEADERSHIP GETS hard, and it can be very lonely. There was a year at Live Original (LO) when three of the ten women who worked on my team left. The reasons were all logical—a husband took a job in a different state, babies were born, new opportunities came—but the upheaval felt heavy to me.

We wound up hiring five new people, and a few days before they were supposed to start working, I thought about this new season and new staff. How could I honor them and honor God? How could I lead well?

I was on an airplane headed for home when God told me to wash their feet. I thought, *Huh? Wash* whose *feet?*

Yes, Jesus famously washed the feet of His disciples just before He was crucified (John 13)—but I was no Jesus. What was God after here? I wasn't afraid that it would be awkward or gross. But it would require me to pour out my heart to people I knew could hurt me and walk away. Okay, maybe I thought it would be a little awkward. But maybe God thought I needed humbling too. I remember asking God, "But what if they hurt me? That will make it hurt worse if I pour my heart out." Sometimes it feels safer to not get close to people.

I felt God respond, *I understand.*

In that moment I realized God truly does understand.

When Jesus washed His disciples' feet, one pair belonged to Judas, the one who would betray Him in the end. Jesus *knew* the guy would betray Him, and yet still He washed his feet. Another pair of feet belonged to Peter, who would hours later deny Him.

4

I felt the Lord say, *Do not reserve your leadership, Sadie. Do not reserve your love.*

The afternoon of the foot-washing was pivotal for me spiritually. The newly formed team worshiped together, prayed together, and cried together. It was powerful. But then things shifted . . . again. One week later someone on my team turned in her two weeks' notice. Again, it was a perfectly understandable reason. But again, my heart was left rather broken. When I sat still with Jesus and cried and prayed and tried to put words to my pain and stress, He said something that shouldn't have shocked me at all: *I get it.*

Of course He did.

Romans 5:7–8 says all there is to say: when we were like Peter—or even Judas—Jesus didn't just wash our feet; He died for us. When we were at our messiest, our flightiest, our neediest, our most selfish, He said, "I love you enough to die for you."

Jesus gets it, way deeper than we do. My teammate did not betray me, and yet it still hurt. But Jesus actually *was* betrayed, and that just makes the love He displayed on the cross even more radical.

He understands our fears, our hurts, our reservations to love.

He knows us.

He gets us.

He loves us still.

He knew *exactly what we were capable of* and still gave everything for us.

HOW TO PUT LOVE FIRST

It's hard to love others well if you are scared that others will hurt you. Love does come with risk, but the reward is what our souls long for. I had someone on my podcast once say, "The only thing I regret in my marriage is the years that I did not love fearlessly." Don't reserve your love today. Let God's radical love for you overflow to others.

GOD OFFERS YOU SALVATION

For I delivered to you as of first importance what I also received:
that Christ died for our sins in accordance with the Scriptures,
that he was buried, that he was raised on the third day in
accordance with the Scriptures. 1 CORINTHIANS 15:3-4

CHRISTIAN

A LOT OF THINGS BRING ME JOY IN LIFE—HEARING HONEY
say, "Da-da," burying an opponent on the basketball court, and playing games with my family all come to mind. But nothing compares to the joy I feel when I see someone grasp the truth of salvation—the truth that through the work of Jesus Christ, God's Son, who came to earth, wrapped Himself in human flesh, and suffered horrific persecution, even unto death on a cross, we have been rescued from sin's eternal punishment. We have been saved from the ravages of this broken world. We have been saved by God. Nothing gets me fired up more than this because nothing has changed my life more than Jesus has—He changed everything for me, and I want everyone else to know Him too.

We often think that the ache we feel in our hearts and souls can be satisfied by a romantic partner or by earning a certain degree or by getting the job we want or by attaining that eight-pack we've been killing ourselves to get—but those things will never do the trick. That ache you feel was created by God. It will only be satisfied in full by Him.

One of my favorite parts of the week is Sunday afternoon, when my father-in-law, Willie, and I teach an evangelism class at church. And one of my favorite passages of Scripture to lean on when teaching that class is 1 Corinthians 15. The apostle Paul wrote to believers who lived in Corinth to remind them of what they believed, and I never get tired of reading those words because they are the perfect summary of what it means to have faith in Christ.

Whether this idea of following Jesus is brand-new to you or you've been walking with Him for years, I want you to read these words from Paul with fresh eyes today:

> I would remind you, brothers, of the gospel I preached to you, which you received, in which you stand, and by which you are being saved, if you hold fast to the word I preached to you—unless you believed in vain.
>
> For I delivered to you as of first importance what I also received: that Christ died for our sins in accordance with the Scriptures, that he was buried, that he was raised on the third day in accordance with the Scriptures. (vv. 1–4)

The literal meaning of the word *gospel* is simply "the good news," and this rundown *is* good news. Our sins have been covered. Our sins have been forgiven. Regardless of who we used to be or what we used to do, we can step into new life right here, right now, and start living for Jesus Christ.

Man, that is beautiful truth.

Do you believe this truth? Have you gone all-in with God?

HOW TO PUT LOVE FIRST

As we think about how to put love first in our lives, consider the saving love of God that put us first. My prayer for you is that you would know the good news of being saved by God, today and every day. If you've never reached out to God for forgiveness and salvation, it's our prayer you'll do that today. That is the true first step of putting love first.

GOD IS YOUR GOOD FATHER

The Spirit himself bears witness with our spirit
that we are children of God. ROMANS 8:16

SADIE

I HAVE AN INCREDIBLE DAD WHO IS NOW A DEAR FRIEND,
but during my middle school and high school years, my dad and I
really struggled to have a great relationship. Honestly, we just missed
out on connecting with each other.

My dad didn't exactly have the best of fatherly role models growing
up—my grandpa has been pretty candid about his harmful decisions
when my dad and his brothers were young. My dad didn't grow up
hearing his dad say "I love you" or "I'm proud of you" or having him
show any affection toward him. And so, in return, there was not a lot
of "I love you" from my dad to me.

Back then, I assumed the reason my dad didn't show me that kind
of affection or give me that kind of affirmation was because *I* was not
enough. So, I started hustling to get my dad's attention, to get him
to notice me, but it felt like no matter what I did, he still missed me.

All throughout the Bible there is imagery of God as our Father
and us as His children, such as in today's verse from Romans 8:16. My
experience with my own dad taught me that whether you have the best
dad on the planet or the absolute worst one, every dad has been ripped
up by the same sin, insecurity, and pain as the rest of us. Every dad
needs the love of a heavenly Father to help him live and lead the way
he should. Dads cannot give what they do not have.

One of the greatest gifts God gave me during those years was a
better understanding of His unconditional love for me. I didn't have to
hustle for God's attention. All that I needed I already had: He was my

Father, and I was His child. And the same is true for you. No matter how incapable your dad is, that is not who God is. And no matter how amazing your dad is, your heavenly Father is greater still.

My dad has always been a Christian and a great man, but when he experienced a radical transformation in his relationship with God, it transformed our relationship. He sent me a long text one time, telling me how proud he was of me and how much he loved me, and I saved it like it was the most momentous thing I'd ever read.

Now I hear the words "I love you" often. He tells me he is proud of me, he hugs me when he sees me, and he even writes me letters! And there it is—he sees me, without me having to strive.

But it is important to note that by the time that happened, I'd already found my footing in my heavenly Father's love, and I no longer ached for anything more. Instead of hoping for attention and affection from my dad as I had before, I started hoping for attention and affection *for* my dad *from* God. He needed to receive God's love to be able to give love away.

The same goes for you and me. We only have love to give others when we've been filled up with the love of God.

ℍ𝕆𝕎 𝕋𝕆 ℙ𝕌𝕋 **LOVE** 𝔽𝕀ℝ𝕊𝕋

If you have a relationship with your dad or other father figure, reach out today with a call, text, or big hug. If that relationship is strained, cover it in prayer today. I encourage you to lean into God's love as the Father He is and let Him fill that gap in your heart.

GOD FORGIVES YOU

But I say, walk by the Spirit, and you will not gratify
the desires of the flesh. GALATIANS 5:16

CHRISTIAN

I DON'T KNOW ABOUT YOU, BUT WHEN I FIRST STARTED
following God, I assumed I would instantly be a completely changed
person, that I would automatically desire the things of God, that I
would walk according to the Spirit and not the ways of the world.
Granted, I was changed—eternally changed. But being changed and
saved doesn't mean we won't still struggle with fleshly desires. They
are part of this broken world.

So if you're an angry person, or struggle with lustful thoughts, or
spend all your time being jealous of people who have nicer things than
you, there's a good chance all of those things didn't turn off immediately after you were saved. We still live in this world, surrounded by
worldly desires—constant reminders of our brokenness.

In Galatians 5:22–23, Paul told us that there is another way to
live, a much more fruitful way to live. "But the fruit of the Spirit is
love, joy, peace, patience, kindness, goodness, faithfulness, gentleness,
self-control."

I read a list like that and think, *I pick that. That's who I want to be.*

You can choose that too. You can become that kind of person. You
can go from being the angriest person alive to being the *gentlest*. You
can go from being lust-filled to being *self-controlled*. You can go from
being the most stressed out to being the absolute model of *peace*.

When we declare that Jesus is Lord of our lives, we are forgiven of
all that we used to be and are invited to become something new. Paul
wrote, "I have been crucified with Christ. It is no longer I who live,

but Christ who lives in me" (Galatians 2:20). When we're "in Christ," Christ lives *in us*. And by the power of His Spirit, He starts living *through us* too.

We need this news, don't we? While we can sit here all day long trying to justify our sin, we're still absolutely guilty of sin.

I couldn't love my wife more than I do. She has the purest heart, she is wise and kind, she is both loving and lovable, and she's a great doubles partner on the tennis court. She's amazing. And yet *even Sadie Robertson Huff has sinned.*

We've *all* been tried, and we've *all* been found guilty—which is precisely what makes the good news of the gospel so good. The question isn't whether we've fallen short of God's standard of perfection; we have. But what do we do about our sin problem?

The forgiveness of God is our only hope. And once we commit ourselves to Jesus and long to "walk by the Spirit," as Paul said, we no longer have to *gratify* those fleshly desires like fits of rage, chronic envy, sexual immorality, or drunken nights.

All of it is forgiven by Jesus. All of it can be washed away. And the ripple effect of walking in the Spirit and not in the flesh will leave every single person who knows and loves you shaking their heads in disbelief at the miracle of God's forgiveness and the Spirit's work in your life.

HOW TO PUT LOVE FIRST

I don't know what you are struggling with today, but God does. Let's pray together today: *Jesus, I love You. Thank You for helping me with* _____. *I give this over to You today.*

GOD HAS COMPASSION FOR YOU

"And he arose and came to his father. But while he was still a long way off, his father saw him and felt compassion, and ran and embraced him and kissed him." LUKE 15:20

SADIE

WHEN HONEY WAS ONE, I HAD A SERIES OF SPEAKING engagements that took me to four states in two days, and while that kind of trip normally wouldn't faze me, this time I was traveling alone with her. And Honey was *busy.*

So on this whirlwind business trip, I was in for it. While I appreciated the instant twenty-pound weight loss every time I put her down, as soon as her little feet touched the ground, she was off. Airport after airport, every time she reached the floor, *whoosh!* Off she went.

I would wonder, *Doesn't she know that she's supposed to stay near me? That it's not safe to run from me? That I'm really not trying to ruin all her fun by having her right by my side, where I can take care of her?*

After Jesus was crucified, His dear friend Peter returned to what he did before he followed Jesus—he went fishing. I know that doesn't seem like a big deal, but with all that Peter had walked through with Jesus, you would think that he would still be preaching the gospel and going around believing for healing and miracles. But nope, he was fishing.

I believe Peter returned to fishing because that was comfortable to him, because before Jesus, that was what Peter did. I wonder if he thought that by denying Jesus and abandoning Him during His darkest hour, he no longer knew what to do, so he just went back to fishing.

But Jesus came back for Peter. He called to him from the shore, gave him a miracle catch of fish, and then sat with him, had a breakfast with him, and redeemed and restored their relationship with three "I love you" moments.

Honey may run when her feet hit the ground, but although she may have to face consequences for running away, I am always going to run after her, pick her up, and tell her that I love her. In the same way, we can chase our own will, running back to what feels good and what is comfortable, or we can surrender to Jesus and run back to God.

> Will you submit yourself to God? He will give you grace.

Will you submit yourself to God? He will give you grace, and just like I do when my Honey comes back to me from her defiant, willful ways, God welcomes us back into His arms.

HOW TO PUT LOVE FIRST

Have you been running from God recently or resting in Him? Sometimes, even after we are saved, we get distracted and tempted to run off. Let's pray together: *God, don't let us run away from You or Your will for us. Help us stay with You.*

GOD DELIGHTS IN YOU

The LORD your God is with you, the Mighty Warrior who saves. He will take great delight in you; in his love he will no longer rebuke you, but will rejoice over you with singing. ZEPHANIAH 3:17 NIV

SADIE

YEARS AGO, AFTER A TERRIBLE BUT NEEDED BREAKUP, I stood in front of the mirror and hated what I saw. It wasn't my body that I hated, but the reality of my life. I was at my lowest point mentally, spiritually, and emotionally—a result of the wildly dysfunctional relationship I'd been in. I cried so hard that I wondered if the tears would ever stop.

Today's verse from Zephaniah popped into mind that night. God was rejoicing over me? Me, with my wayward heart, my scattered thoughts, my out-of-control emotions, and my mascara-smudged eyes? As difficult as it was for me to believe, He was.

I'd spent nearly three years working like crazy to please and delight my boyfriend, and I'd failed. Nothing was ever enough. And yet here was God, looking at me in my worst-possible condition, saying, "You're delightful to Me."

I remember being so perplexed by that idea. *I was delightful, in that state, to God?*

Something hit me that night that I've never forgotten: God doesn't delight in us because we're especially delightful; He delights in us because we are *His.*

We need this message today! A lot of us think that the acceptance and comfort and love we're seeking are going to come through a relationship, but they're not. They come only through our relationship with Christ. We are always enough for Him.

After that bad breakup, it would have been easy to wake up each day feeling unhappy over what had just ended. But I chose instead to wake up seeking the will of God. I started each day begging God to keep me from feeling bitter and angry and jealous. Day after day I asked Him to help me feel love, gratitude, and peace. I started praying for my ex instead of despising him. I looked for ways I could learn from the experience instead of wishing it had never happened.

Over time, as I was consistent about seeking God's will and practicing God's ways, He started showing me a picture of the man He had for me. This man would be tender and kind. He would be funny. He would compel me toward deeper intimacy with Jesus through his unwavering acceptance and love.

I caught some flak for what looked like flying through guys as I dated and moved on quickly. But the truth was that God had given me a picture of the type of man who was worth waiting for, and those guys just weren't my husband. By the time I met Christian, I was so sure that he was the man God had for me that I felt instantly at peace with him. He was not perfect—no one is. I sure am not! But there was a peace. The irony of this story is that I really began to find love at a time when it looked like I'd lost it. It was when I was single that I began to find love—God's love.

If I could give you one piece of advice as you're dealing with pain or heartbreak—which is always part of life—it's to start taking God's Word personally. The Bible is a love letter from our heavenly Father to us, a love letter from One who delights in us. He sees you. He loves you. He has good plans for you. He rejoices over you and lifts your spirits with His song.

HOW TO PUT **LOVE** FIRST

Let the reminder that God delights in you and rejoices over you wash over you today. Write it down, repeat it to yourself, say it out loud.

GOD HEALS YOU

"For I will restore health to you, and your wounds I
will heal, declares the LORD." JEREMIAH 30:17

SADIE

MY FAMILY EXPERIENCED A DIVINE HEALING WHEN MY grandfather—whom we call 2-Papa—was diagnosed with stage 4 colorectal cancer. His doctor said he had three to six months to live.

That was twenty years ago, and not only is he still a very present man in my life, but he's logging his ten thousand steps every day.

God can restore our health, and He can heal our wounds (Jeremiah 30:17). And yet I find healing baffling because it doesn't always happen *right this minute*, the way we want it to. God often heals over time, and other times He doesn't heal at all this side of heaven.

One summer I swapped DMs with Jane Marczewski, known to the *America's Got Talent* audience as Nightbirde. When she auditioned for the show, she told the judges that she'd spent years battling cancer but was excited to sing for them a song she'd written, titled "It's Okay." Her performance was so moving that it earned Jane the rare "golden buzzer" from Simon Cowell, which meant she was automatically put through to the competition's semifinals. I reached out to tell her how impactful her audition had been and that we all were cheering for her to beat cancer. We texted here and there as she continued to battle cancer and adjust to fame. I was so impressed by her warmth and energy and crazy-strong faith that I just *knew* God was going to heal her.

But that's not what He did. Halfway through the season, Jane pulled out of the competition because her cancer had gotten much worse. Six months later, she was gone.

Baffling, right?

There are no easy answers here, so I won't try to toss one your way. What I will do is remind you that even the greatest heroes of the faith have shaken their heads in disbelief over some of the decisions God made. In Hebrews 11 there's this amazing rundown of faithful people like Abel, Enoch, Noah, Abraham, Isaac, Jacob, and Sarah. They are listed in what's known as the "hall of faith." And yet in verse 13 of that same chapter, it says, "These all died in faith, not having received the things promised."

Wait. What? These were the best-of-the-best lovers and followers of God, and God chose *not* to deliver on His promises to them? But then verse 16 says, "But as it is, they [those faithful ones] desire a better country, that is, a heavenly one. Therefore God . . . has prepared for them a city."

God also prepared a place for Jane. One that has joy in fullness, love in fullness, and health in fullness. No more sickness.

If you're waiting for healing in some part of your life—whether it's physical, relational, financial, job-related, church-related, emotional, or something else entirely—I want to remind you that God has not forgotten you. He holds all healing in His hand. And whether He chooses to heal you here and now, or whether the great things He has in store for you will show up in heaven someday, three things remain totally true: God is still God. God is good. And God has a plan for your life.

HOW TO PUT LOVE FIRST

What healing do you need today? Whatever it is, and whether it's for you or someone you dearly love, let's go to our Father. *Jesus, we lay down _____. We both ask and thank You for Your healing. In Your name, amen.*

GOD CALLS YOU TO GREAT THINGS

Only let each person lead the life that the Lord has assigned to him, and to which God has called him. 1 CORINTHIANS 7:17

CHRISTIAN

GROWING UP IN THE CHURCH I ALWAYS HEARD ABOUT people being "called" by God, like there was a giant cell phone in heaven that He would use to convey a message to someone on earth. If God had called me back then, I'm not sure I would have wanted to answer. It seemed like most of the people who were called got sent out as missionaries to far-flung places around the world. I liked Florida. I didn't see any reason to leave. If I minded my business, maybe God would reach out to someone else.

As I grew in my faith, I started to understand more about His "divine calling." In actuality, being *called by God* isn't something that's reserved for a special few. Everyone is called by God.

The Bible talks about two kinds of callings: first, God issues a call to everyone on the planet, that they would believe in His Son, Jesus, and invite Jesus into their hearts. Whenever someone in Scripture is compelled to follow Jesus, they are responding to God's universal "call." In the book of Acts, the apostle Peter told a huge group of people who were curious about Jesus: "Repent and be baptized every one of you in the name of Jesus Christ for the forgiveness of your sins, and you will receive the gift of the Holy Spirit" (Acts 2:38). The call went out and people responded.

God wants *everyone* to repent of their sins and to trust Jesus for forgiveness. That's the first calling from God.

The second calling is reserved for those who choose to say yes.

Just before Jesus left the earth to return to heaven, He told His followers what He wanted them to do while He was gone: "All authority in heaven and on earth has been given to me. Go therefore and make disciples of all nations, baptizing them in the name of the Father and of the Son and of the Holy Spirit, teaching them to observe all that I have commanded you. And behold, I am with you always, to the end of the age" (Matthew 28:18–20). This set of instructions is called the Great Commission, and it's the calling on every believer's life. We are supposed to help others find and follow Jesus by teaching them all that we've learned.

If you're a Christian who plays sports, then while you're pursuing your sports career, you're helping others find and follow Jesus.

If you're a Christian who loves numbers and works in accounting, then while you're going about your business, you're helping others find and follow Jesus.

If you're a pastor who works in a church, then while you're doing vocational ministry, you're helping others find and follow Jesus. (Hopefully, that one's a given!)

Whatever you're pursuing as a believer, your calling is always the same: Help people find Jesus. Help people follow Jesus.

HOW TO PUT LOVE FIRST

Do you feel like you are living and serving in your second calling? *God, today in our work or in our play, help us reach out to someone for You.*

GOD'S DISCIPLINE LEADS YOU TO RIGHTEOUSNESS

For the moment all discipline seems painful rather than pleasant, but later it yields the peaceful fruit of righteousness to those who have been trained by it. HEBREWS 12:11

CHRISTIAN

ON THE FIRST DAY OF THIRD GRADE, I HAD TO TAKE A READing comprehension test to see if I should be in the normal class or in the class for the more advanced kids. I remember it like it was yesterday—sitting at my little desk, pulling out my pencil, and resolving in my heart that I was going to ace this thing. I was going to do whatever I could to get into that advanced-kid class.

If my memory serves me well, I scored a forty—as in forty out of *one hundred.*

Not good.

From that day forward, I arrived early at school to meet with my English teacher, determined to read better and faster. She'd always start by handing me one of those guided reading strips that highlights one portion of text at a time. I'd sit there under her watchful eye, making out letters, words, syllables, sentences.

It was difficult, but I persevered. I wanted to read that badly. This discipline continued into sports and later into fitness training.

When Sadie and I met with that life coach, I was kind of in awe. That guy is a *machine.* He gets up at four-thirty every morning and spends an hour reading the Bible. He's always asking God, "What's Your input here? What's Your counsel there? Which way should I go?"

Then at five-thirty, he hops on a stationary spin bike and rides for an hour. And *then* he starts his day. He says he hasn't used an alarm in decades because his body is tuned in to this flow.

Did I mention he's in his sixties?

All I know is when I grow up, I want to be just like him. He's happy. He's centered. He's productive. He's kind. And as I scrutinize his lifestyle, I think that discipline is the culprit.

In Hebrews 12, the writer acknowledged that being disciplined isn't always fun. "For the moment all discipline seems painful rather than pleasant." That's some truth, right there: painful rather than pleasant. And yet it's worth it, in the end. He goes on: "But later it [discipline] yields the peaceful fruit of righteousness to those who have been trained by it" (v. 11).

Did you catch that—the "peaceful fruit of righteousness" part?

I don't mean to be presumptuous, but I think that's what you and I are after here. We want peace. We want fruitfulness. We want right living.

I don't know where you fall on the discipline spectrum. I'm not here to judge you or convince you to adopt a four-thirty wake-up call. What I *am* here to do is encourage you to be disciplined in the things of God.

Here's where we begin: When in your ridiculously busy day do you stop to read God's Word?

Sort it out now, at least for today. When will you sit and read God's Word? What time will you talk to this Father you say you've given yourself to?

Begin there, and then just see what unfolds. If you're like me, you'll discover that discipline begets discipline.

HOW TO PUT LOVE FIRST

If you are starting from scratch here, begin with at least five minutes of prayer and five minutes of Bible reading today. Even this small amount can have a huge impact.

GOD ADOPTS YOU

"And I will be a father to you, and you shall be sons and daughters to me, says the Lord Almighty." 2 CORINTHIANS 6:18

SADIE

WHEN I WAS SIXTEEN YEARS OLD, MY FAMILY WENT TO HAITI to visit an orphanage filled with boys and girls who, for one reason or another, had lost their families. It was the sixth year in a row that I'd been to the developing world, and I was still struck by how hard the realities of poverty and famine hit children. They had little protection from what must have felt like a very cruel world.

One boy I met in Haiti was a two-year-old who went by the name Moses because he'd been found abandoned at the river's edge. His eyes were yellow from lack of nutrition, his belly was distended, and his body was filled with disease. The staff at the orphanage informed us he wouldn't let anyone hold him. But the second he saw me, he came over and reached his arms up for me to hold him and said, "Mama."

I wanted so badly to bring him home with me. I didn't even care that I was only sixteen. I did not want to leave Moses. But I had to. Years later I got to bring Christian to Haiti to meet Moses, and they had the sweetest bond. Moses will always hold a special place in our hearts, and he gave us the desire to adopt one day.

In my family, I have more adopted siblings than biological ones. My mom and dad share in their love for adoption and for bringing kids to forever families. They love all of us kids the same despite our differences. Our home life was never perfect—far from it. But we were a family full of diversity and full of love.

Maybe you are reading this right now, and you're not sure how this relates to you. Galatians 4:4–7 says, "But when the fullness of time had come, God sent forth his Son, born of woman, born under the law, to redeem those who were under the law, so that we might receive adoption as sons. And because you are sons, God has sent the Spirit of his Son into our hearts, crying, 'Abba! Father!' So you are no longer a slave, but a son, and if a son, then an heir through God."

> The amazing thing is, everyone is loved the same in God's family.

If you have accepted Jesus Christ into your life, then you are in the family of God. And the amazing thing is, everyone is loved the same in God's family. Every one of us is loved wildly enough that God would send Jesus to die in our place. It doesn't matter what your background is—you are His.

You matter in this family.

HOW TO PUT LOVE FIRST

Adoption is messy, hard—and an amazingly beautiful gift. Let's put ourselves out there today to make a meaningful connection with adoption in some capacity. This could be donating to a cause, offering to help an adoptive family, or opening our hearts to what God might have for us.

DAY 12

GOD TRANSFORMS YOU

And we all, with unveiled face, beholding the glory of the
Lord, are being transformed into the same image from
one degree of glory to another. 2 CORINTHIANS 3:18

SADIE

HAVE YOU EVER BEEN WITH A GROUP OF PEOPLE TELLING
their testimonies and felt a little insecure about yours not being as epic?
I have definitely felt that way. I mean, I have never been in prison for
some crazy crime. I've never been strung out on heroin or cocaine. I've
never slept around. I've never even been drunk. It has made me wonder
if my story is even worth telling.

Here is the thing, friends. Even though I was not as wild and
crazy as some of my peers in my younger days, *I was still lost.* I was
deeply insecure. My thought life was overtaking me. I was drowning
in anxiety. I was obsessive about every calorie I ate, to the point of a
disorder. I was way too invested in a dysfunctional relationship. And
although I did not have sex before marriage, I wasn't exactly pure. At
the time I couldn't even admit the awful state I was in because I knew
if I did, I'd have to change. As long as I was comparing my sin to the
sins of others and not the holiness of Christ, my sin didn't seem so bad.

No matter how many stories I hear from people about the specific
ways God has rocked their world, one theme runs through them all:
they once were blind in some aspect of life, but then after meeting
Jesus, they could see.

This happened for the apostle Paul when he encountered Jesus.
Paul, who at the time was called Saul, was headed for the city of
Damascus, where he was planning to capture and imprison believ-
ers. But Jesus interrupted his journey and gave him a different plan.

Acts 9:8–9 says that after the shock and awe of being knocked to the ground by Jesus, "Saul rose from the ground, and although his eyes were opened, he saw nothing. So they led him by the hand and brought him into Damascus. And for three days he was without sight, and neither ate nor drank."

Then God sent a man named Ananias to be His spokesperson in Saul's life. Ananias said, "'Brother Saul, the Lord Jesus who appeared to you on the road by which you came has sent me so that you may regain your sight and be filled with the Holy Spirit.' And immediately something like scales fell from his eyes, and he regained his sight. Then he rose and was baptized; and taking food, he was strengthened" (vv. 17–19).

Saul then went to the synagogues in town—not to harm anyone as he had planned to do, but to help heal them by telling them that Jesus was Lord. Saul went from being a murderer to being a missionary for the cause of Christ. That is pretty epic!

My story isn't as radical as Paul's, but it's still epic in the transformation I experienced. The same grace has saved me and set me free. I was blind, but now I see.

Once I gave my life to Jesus fully, I let His Spirit lead me, and I began to get my life straight. If you're struggling in life and don't know where to begin, begin with Jesus. His grace is sufficient.

Let Jesus in and transformation will start taking hold in your life.

HOW TO PUT LOVE FIRST

Today, let's write out our testimonies. There's power when we put pen to paper, and now we'll have a written record to return to when we need a reminder of what God has done for us.

GOD MAKES YOU SECURE

[God] saved us and called us to a holy calling, not because of
our works but because of his own purpose and grace, which he
gave us in Christ Jesus before the ages began. 2 TIMOTHY 1:9

SADIE

IT IS NO SECRET THAT I HAVE A BIG PERSONALITY. IF YOU
have ever met me, listened to my podcast, or heard me preach, then
you know I am very passionate about every word I am saying. Christian
is also passionate, but in a much more subtle way. He doesn't talk as
much as I do, and he sure doesn't talk with his hands like I do.

When we were dating, I was talking with an older couple who I
viewed as mentors about how in love I was with my soon-to-be fiancé
and how amazing I thought our differences were. After all my swoon-
ing, the husband looked at me with this piercing gaze and said, "You
and Christian will have a decade-long struggle over his not knowing
what his purpose in life should be. He will always feel like his dreams
are less important than yours. He'll always feel like his personality is
smaller than yours. He'll feel like he is in your shadow."

I tried to say something in response, but my face was frozen. I
just stood there in shock, having no clue what to do. A million hypo-
theticals flooded my mind. We were in for a decade-long struggle?
Christian wouldn't know his life purpose because of *me*? Were my
dreams too big? Should my dreams even be my dreams? Was I about
to consign him to insecurity all his life?

I sat with all those doubts and questions for a few minutes,
wrestling with each of them to try to get to the truth. Then I remembered what Christian said to me when we started dating and I was

about to go on tour: "If it's a win for God's kingdom and a win for you, then it's a win for me too."

Christian was so confident, so humble, so secure in Jesus, that I realized I did not have to accept that man's words as truth. I could be *aware* of this opinion without being *afraid* of it. This was a conversation that would help Christian and me continue to grow our security in Christ. My boyfriend wasn't looking to the world or to me for his security. He was looking only to God. He knew that God calls each of us to a specific purpose "which he gave us in Christ Jesus before the ages began" (2 Timothy 1:9).

If our security is found in our abilities, opportunities, positions, job titles, relationships, financial status, or any other external thing, then the loss of those things will shake us. If our security is found in others' approval, then comments like the one I was given will make us insecure. But if we find our security in God alone, a God who never changes and whose words about us never change, our security won't change either.

We can feel secure 100 percent of the time when our security comes from Him. Now that is the way to live!

HOW TO PUT LOVE FIRST

Most of us go through seasons where we find our security in something or someone other than God, but our capacity to love and love well can grow exponentially when our security is grounded in Christ. Today, let's name the people and things that our security strays to, and then let's ask God to help us find our security in Him.

GOD WANTS YOUR PERSISTENCE

Pursue a righteous life—a life of wonder, faith, love, steadiness, courtesy. Run hard and fast in the faith. Seize the eternal life, the life you were called to. 1 TIMOTHY 6:11–12 MSG

CHRISTIAN

ONE NIGHT AS SADIE AND I WERE GETTING SETTLED TO watch a movie, I noticed that my back was wrenching up. "You know, you could always just take tomorrow off," Sadie suggested.

Off from running, she meant. Off from training ridiculously hard toward this goal I was trying to hit. If you follow the CrossFit community, you may remember when a guy named Adam Klink caused quite a stir when he did a single-rep five-hundred-pound back squat and ran a sub-five-minute mile on the same day.

A few weeks earlier I had participated in a competition where I benched 315 pounds, deadlifted 515 pounds, and back squatted 500. It took me three years of dedicated training to get to those numbers, and once I hit that back squat, I figured that I should train for the sub-five mile.

Did I mention I hate running? Or cardio training of any kind?

Despite Sadie's completely reasonable suggestion to take a day off, I knew if I didn't force myself to stick to my training schedule, I'd slouch around doing nothing productive and blame it all on my back.

If I want the benefits of persistence, I've got to keep at it. This isn't just true for my life physically; it's also true for me spiritually. I won't grow and mature in my faith if I take time off and slack.

I started the *4:8 Men* podcast for one purpose—to encourage guys to train both physically and spiritually in life. In 1 Timothy 4:8, the verse that my podcast is named after, Paul explained how to train for righteousness: "For while bodily training is of some value, godliness is of value in every way, as it holds promise for the present life and also for the life to come." Paul was telling believers that spiritual fitness requires training, and it requires much more work and has much more value than bodily training.

Listen, I will be crazy-thrilled if I'm actually able to hit that 500/5 goal. But even as I train for that physical feat, I'm always thinking about my spiritual life. In the same way that I'm not *naturally* a strong person or a fast person, I'm not a good person or a moral person or a pure person. I don't naturally want to read the Bible, pray, or consider other people's needs above my own. In my flesh, I'm one sorry dude.

But with training, I can want different things; I can become more like Christ.

So, I fight and I train. I fight for my faith. I train for my family. I persist to stay the course with Jesus, so that I will be strong in spirit and ready for when that fitness is tested.

I wish I could tell you that you could make the decision to follow Jesus once and then kind of coast from there on out, but that isn't the case. We have to *actively persist* in our faith. Ask yourself if you're actively training today, or if you're aimlessly meandering. The blessings of persistence are waiting for you.

HOW TO PUT LOVE FIRST

Today, as you do a physical activity—maybe it's a run, or a trip to the gym, or some yoga or stretching—try to memorize 1 Timothy 4:8 and think of persisting spiritually as you work physically.

GOD REDEEMS YOUR SCARS

For if you live according to the flesh you will die, but if by the Spirit you put to death the deeds of the body, you will live. ROMANS 8:13

SADIE

NOT MANY PEOPLE KNOW THIS ABOUT ME, BUT WHEN I WAS sixteen years old, I got in a moped accident. You don't think about how much damage a little moped can do to you, but I flipped off of it at about forty miles per hour on a busy highway in Florida. I could have died, but by the grace of God, I walked away with a lot of scrapes and bruises that have now turned into scars on my body.

One of my favorite parts of the story of Jesus' resurrection is such a small detail that it's easy to miss. In John 20, we read that Jesus went to the place where His disciples were to tell them He was alive. He walked into the room and said, "Peace be with you" (v. 19). Then He "showed them his hands and his side" (v. 20). They could see the evidence of His torture and the excruciating pain of being hung on a cross.

> The scars on His hands and ankles and side were a testimony to God's power at work in His life. *And the same is true for us.*

The part I love is that Jesus still had scars. This might not seem like a big deal, but to me that little detail gives us deep and abiding hope. Jesus' scars showed that He'd been through the worst of times—He was truly dead and buried—and yet three days later He was with the disciples and fully *alive*. The scars on His hands and ankles and side were a testimony to God's power at work in His life. *And the same is true for us.*

I know life can be rough. Some seasons can be really hard, and we come out of them with more than a few scars. To have a scar means that pain was a part of the story. Sometimes the scars are from our own doing, a result of the sin in our pasts. It can be hard to sit with that reality, even though we know everyone has sinned and fallen short of the glory of God.

But here's what I want you to know: those scars you bear can serve as a powerful testimony too. In Romans 8:13–14, the apostle Paul said that "if by the Spirit you put to death the misdeeds of the body, you will live. For those who are led by the Spirit of God are the children of God" (NIV). I have scars on my hands and on my stomach from that moped accident, but when I look at them, I am not reminded of the pain; I am reminded of the time God saved me. Likewise, I have spiritual scars in my heart, but when I think of them, it is not pain that I feel, but grace that is unending and love that has healed me.

God knows we are all a mess. We are sin-riddled, wayward children, and only by the grace of God are we lifted up and made new. He pulls us out of our mess with our scars still showing and allows us to say, "I used to be held by sin and selfishness, but now I'm held by God's grace."

If you are living devoted to Jesus, you're eternally held by God's grace.

HOW TO PUT LOVE FIRST

It's rarely our natural and first reaction to love our scars and blemishes, both internal and external. *God, we give You our scars today, and we ask that You help us see Your beauty and grace in them. Amen.*

GOD FULFILLS AND SATISFIES YOU

"Blessed are those who hunger and thirst for righteousness, for they shall be satisfied." MATTHEW 5:6

CHRISTIAN

I HEARD A LINE RECENTLY THAT I LOVED: "A DOZEN DONUTS will never taste as good as being fit feels." That's some truth right there. That line of thinking is what helps me get up early, despite having slept barely three hours because I was up all night with Honey. It's what compels me to stuff workout gear into my duffel every time Sadie and I head out of town, resolved to hit the gym even while on the road. It's what makes me push through the aches and pains that pop up and stay the course with the fitness plan I've set.

> Feeling spiritually fit is even more satisfying than feeling physically fit.

I didn't fully grasp this until a few years ago, but feeling spiritually fit is even more satisfying than feeling physically fit. And just like saying no to donuts and yes to the gym helps my body's fitness, saying no to sin and committing to righteous living feeds and fills my spirit. Who knew?

I know from experience that sin isn't all it's cracked up to be. Notice I didn't say sin's not fun. Sin can be *ridiculously* fun. But the fleeting fun, the temporary high, the brief adrenaline that sin gives us is super short-lived. And the low that comes right after that high starts to crest? It's a killer every time.

One of my best friends in college was my roommate my junior year, and while I loved the guy like a brother, our pasts could not have been more different. Early on I had been the party guy, always up for a night out, always chasing the high—even while I was involved at church. My roommate was the opposite. He was the well-rounded, thoughtful, studious kind of guy who was actually at college to *go to school*. (Novel idea, right?)

Recently I was thinking back on a conversation that he and I had while living together that junior year. He knew that I'd been wild before but that my life was different now, and one night while we were talking, he said, "Christian, I'm glad you've been open and honest about how empty those days were for you. I have to admit, sometimes I felt like I was missing out on all the 'fun' stuff. You've helped me never question my choices again."

My friend had missed out on *nothing*. I'd been the one to miss out because only Jesus can fill what needs filling in our lives. Only He can satisfy. The beautiful thing is that when we let Him play that role for us instead of chasing fulfillment in futile ways, we come to our relationships already filled up. Instead of needing validation or support or affection, we come eager to serve and to love.

HOW TO PUT **LOVE** FIRST

What's one of the things you're running to for fulfillment instead of running to God? Social media? A person? Actual donuts? Today, let's name the thing and lay it down for twenty-four hours. Today, I'm fasting from _____ and praying and reading God's Word instead.

GOD SPEAKS TO YOU

"Call to me and I will answer you, and will tell you great and hidden things that you have not known." JEREMIAH 33:3

SADIE

AFTER CHRISTIAN AND I GOT MARRIED, WE RECEIVED A joint job offer that blew both of our minds. It was an exciting opportunity with a great ministry, but we'd have to move to another state. We weren't planning to move again, considering we had just moved back to Louisiana. So we agreed to pray about it before we gave a firm answer.

As both of us separately prayed for direction, we kept hearing one word: *No*. But then we started questioning ourselves. Were we *sure* we'd heard from God? It was an amazing opportunity after all, and we would be crazy to say no to it.

We prayed more and asked God to make it abundantly clear.

Still, the answer was no.

Then, as if to confirm what He'd already communicated, God made it even clearer: we found out we were pregnant with our first baby. We weren't expecting to get pregnant so early, but we both knew we wanted to raise our kids near family, so we decided to stay. I'm so glad that we leaned in and trusted God with that decision. We now know He was speaking loud and clear.

When I was trying to think of a favorite example in Scripture of God speaking to somebody, I had to laugh. Pretty much *every* story in the Bible involves God talking to His people and asking them to step out of their comfort zones. But here is one I love: Before Jesus came to earth, a teenage girl named Mary was told that she would bear a child, which had to have been shocking. But equally shocking was when

Mary's fiancé, Joseph, learned that she was pregnant. Since they hadn't had sex yet, he wondered how she was pregnant.

But Joseph was a righteous man. To avoid bringing shame to Mary, he planned to cancel the wedding quietly and have them go their separate ways. While he was thinking things through, an angel of the Lord came to Joseph in a dream and filled him in on what had happened. "Joseph, son of David," the angel said, "do not fear to take Mary as your wife, for that which is conceived in her is from the Holy Spirit. She will bear a son, and you shall call his name Jesus, for he will save his people from their sins" (Matthew 1:20–21).

Joseph woke up, probably totally confused about what he'd heard. But he took God at His word and did what he'd been told, even though it did not make sense at the time. He took Mary as his wife, caring for her as she brought Jesus into the world.

I want to make you two promises right now: First, if you will ask God to start speaking to you, He will answer that prayer with a yes. And that may not be in an audible voice or in the timing you expect, but He will speak. Just like Jeremiah 33:3 says, He *loves* to engage with His children and tell us things we didn't yet know. Second, as you're faithful to listen for His promptings, you'll get better at detecting His voice. You'll need to spend time dwelling in His presence and learning to discern, but He will speak and you will know it.

HOW TO PUT LOVE FIRST

Sometimes remembering God's past faithfulness encourages us in the present and for the future. Today, let's remember (and tell someone!) about a time we *know* God spoke to us or gave us guidance. If you have never had that happen, ask God for guidance today. His guidance will always align with His Word.

GOD PROMOTES YOU FOR HIS GLORY

"But seek first his kingdom and his righteousness, and all these things will be given to you as well." MATTHEW 6:33 NIV

CHRISTIAN

WHEN I GRADUATED FROM COLLEGE, I WAS KIND OF UNSURE about what I wanted to do next. I was glad to be done with school and to have earned a degree, but there was no obvious path forward, nothing I was sure I wanted to do. I had studied business management. I liked pretty much every sport. I loved God. I loved Sadie by that point too. But in terms of making those variables fit into some nice, neat equation for success, I was at a loss.

I was tempted a few times to anxiously wonder about my future. But I kept coming back to the idea that if I focused on my relationship with God more than I focused on finding a job, things would take care of themselves.

Some of the most influential people in the Bible—the ones who have most dramatically shaped our faith—are a bunch of people who weren't exactly top-notch candidates any hiring manager would choose today. Moses, the great Hebrew leader, wouldn't even get an interview because of the homicide of an Egyptian on his record. David, the guy who eventually became king of Israel, would be eyed with even greater suspicion: *You killed a man to hide the fact that you slept with his wife?* Daniel would get the interview but would probably be seen as a weirdo, with all his talk about interpreting dreams. The apostle Paul would have to explain why he had been on a mission to kill people who had done nothing wrong to him.

The list goes on, but the point is that these days we tend to think we have to have a special talent or ability or skill set to do something important in life. We think we have to chart a course and know exactly where it will lead. But if we want to find real meaning in life, the only thing we need to do is commit ourselves to the Lord. That's what all those biblical figures have in common, you know: for all the dramatic stuff they went through, in the end they wanted to please God. And so God used their lives to radically change the world.

Once Sadie and I got married and relocated to Louisiana, opportunities started coming my way that I could never have orchestrated on my own. I look at what I'm involved in today—with my podcast, with Sadie's ministry, with our church, with our extended family, with people and groups and rec leagues in the community—and I can see God's fingerprints all over everything. Here's what I want you to know, if you're wrestling with what to do next: when you want to influence the world for God, you'll influence the world for good. God will make sure of it.

He knows you.

He's going to use you.

And He's going to promote you for His glory, His gain.

HOW TO PUT LOVE FIRST

God has so many opportunities out there for you, but that may mean you have to go out and get them. A lot of times when we are praying for God to move, He is waiting on *us* to move. So go seek out opportunities to share and serve Him today. Maybe that is through a job interview, asking someone to lunch, or orchestrating a movie night with friends.

GOD SEARCHES FOR YOU

For the eyes of the LORD run to and fro throughout the
whole earth, to give strong support to those whose
heart is blameless toward him. 2 CHRONICLES 16:9

SADIE

IF YOU HAVE HEARD ME PREACH, THEN YOU PROBABLY KNOW
I love Wonder Woman. I have at least five different Wonder Woman
analogies that I can preach anytime, anywhere, anyplace, to anyone
who will listen.

There is a scene in the movie where Steve is taking Diana to where
the German leaders are, but in order to get there, they have to go
through a really bad part of the battlefield. As Steve and the other
guys are walking right past people who are hurting and dying, trying
to get to their destination, Diana stops, insisting that she help. Steve
basically says, "No, it is not even possible to help this situation; it is
no-man's-land. This is not what we came here to do." Diana replies,
"No, but it is what I am going to do."

You and I aren't exactly Wonder Woman, and I'm guessing the
likelihood that we'll face a situation where the entire world's safety
rests on our shoulders sits somewhere around zero percent. But there
are plenty of opportunities to stand up for what is right, for what
will honor God most. And many times it won't be easy. The scene I
described gives me chills because it is such a strong example of someone standing up for what's right, despite the consequences, and it
matters to her because people matter.

When I was just getting to know Christian, one of the aspects of
his character that attracted me was his insistence on doing the right
thing. One time we were with a group of people, and someone started

bad-mouthing a guy who wasn't there. Instead of staying silent or going along with the conversation so that he wouldn't offend anyone, Christian spoke up. "Hey, you don't know him. Don't talk about him like that, all right?"

His remark seemed to steal all the oxygen in the room, and for a minute the entire group stood there in awkward silence, wondering what to do next. But I loved that about him. If Christian would protect his friend like that, I could trust that he would protect me.

When we decide that we can't simply stand by while someone is disparaged, or suffers, or keeps on believing lies, I think God says, "Now *there's* someone whose heart I can trust."

There will always be people like Steve in our lives, people who want us to preserve the status quo, people who are afraid that our words or actions might be misunderstood or canceled or spark controversy. But to follow Jesus is to risk upsetting the system. It's to have conviction for what's right. It's to say, "If nobody else is going to step in and help, then I must."

One of the prophets God sent to remind His people of His truth said that "the eyes of the Lord run to and fro throughout the whole earth, to give strong support to those whose heart is blameless toward him" (2 Chronicles 16:9). Just think: As you act on conviction and do the right thing, God's eyes will land on you. God's strong support will come to you. God will work His plan of redemption through your actions in the world.

HOW TO PUT LOVE FIRST

Who is being ignored or overlooked in your world? Stand up and speak up for the people around you. Welcome them in. Their feelings are worth the awkward moment it will take to do the right thing.

GOD WANTS YOU TO BE READY

"At midnight the cry rang out: 'Here's the bridegroom!
Come out to meet him!'" MATTHEW 25:6 NIV

SADIE

WHEN I REMEMBER BACK TO ALL THE PREPARATION AND self-care I went through for our wedding, I can't help but laugh at some of the things I did in order to be the bride I wanted to be. I worked out with a trainer, I made sure my nails, hair, and tan were perfect—I even waxed my armpits! The things we do for love. But even though a lot of our wedding preparation is silliness, it is a beautiful thing to think that Jesus compared a bride's preparation for a wedding to the preparation of His coming.

Weddings were very different in Jesus' Jewish culture than they are now because the bride did not know what day her wedding would be. It could be tomorrow or two months from now, all depending on when the bridegroom returned, and so she had to stay ready.

In Matthew 25 Jesus told a story of ten bridesmaids. If a girl were asked to be a bridesmaid back then, she would have had to prepare each day as if that could be the day that the bridegroom returned. The job of these girls was to light the way for the bridegroom's return, and so they had to keep their lamps filled with oil for the exciting day.

Matthew 25 tells us that five of them were foolish and five of them were wise. When the foolish girls took their lamps, they took no oil with them, but the wise took oil with their lamps. Though the bridegroom was delayed, finally, at midnight, there was a cry: "Here is the bridegroom! Come meet him." Then all of the bridesmaids rose and trimmed their lamps. The foolish said to the wise, "Give us some of your oil, for our lamps are going to go out" (v. 8).

Being ready requires individual preparation. You need oil to light your lamp, and they did not have any, so they weren't ready when the bridegroom appeared. Oil doesn't just come to you; it is something you have to intentionally go get. My jeep had the oil light on for months until finally it switched from a little light to a big light that said, "Oil change required."

> **Being ready requires individual preparation. You need oil to light your lamp.**

In the same way, in our spiritual lives we have to make sure that we are taking the time to fill our souls with oil. Although the spray tans and waxing weren't exactly necessary, there were other things that were necessary as Christian and I prepared for our marriage that we still see the fruit of, like our devotions with each other, our time in premarital counseling, and every date we went on to laugh and cry and grow closer together.

Your oil light might be going off in your spirit right now. It may be telling you it is time to go do some of the intentional work to be with Jesus. You can keep ignoring it, but it won't go away; eventually things will start to fall apart. Take the time today to go get your oil so that you can truly be a light in the world.

HOW TO PUT LOVE FIRST

Rather than treating it as another item on our to-do list, let's schedule time with God like it's the most important thing on our calendar. Prepare a quiet room or corner. Get a cup of coffee or tea, and prepare to meet Him like you'd meet a special date or your best friend.

GOD GIVES YOU HIS WORD

Take up the whole armor of God, that you may be able to withstand in the evil day. . . . And take the helmet of salvation, and the sword of the Spirit, which is the word of God. EPHESIANS 6:13, 17 NKJV

SADIE

THE FIRST TIME CHRISTIAN EVER CAME TO SEE ME SPEAK ON a tour, he came to the backstage area where all of the speakers, musicians, and show organizers were hanging out. I was thrilled to see him and didn't notice anything weird, but one of the guys came up to him and jokingly said, "You trying to look super-spiritual, or what?"

I looked at Christian and died laughing. I saw what the guy meant. Christian was wearing a T-shirt that had a giant cross on the front of it and was carrying his huge, leather-bound Bible under his arm like he was going to be asked to preach that night.

Not missing a beat, Christian just smiled that winning smile and said, "Hey, man, I always have my sword on me."

It's true. Christian *always* has his Bible on him. He carries it everywhere he goes. When he was shifting gears from living by his own set of rules to living by God's rules, he started taking Bible verses more seriously. Two verses that really motivated him were Hebrews 4:12, which says that God's Word is "living and active, sharper than any two-edged sword, piercing to the division of soul and of spirit, of joints and of marrow, and discerning the thoughts and intentions of the heart," and Ephesians 6:17, which says that as you're putting on the armor of God to withstand each day, you shouldn't forget to take the "sword of the Spirit, which is the word of God."

Armed with these verses, Christian has confidence to move through his day knowing what God wants for him and how to relate to other people. If we want our relationships to work like God desires them to work, we need His wisdom to tell us what to say and do.

How do we respond to rudeness?

How do we handle a sibling who hurt our feelings?

What are the right words to use to gently confront our spouse?

How much do we "own" in a friendship conflict?

We face situations like these every single day, and yet we often are clueless about our thoughts, words, and actions. Fortunately, God's Word has the answers. Proverbs 7:1–3 says, "My son, keep my words and treasure up my commandments with you . . . keep my teaching as the apple of your eye; bind them on your fingers; write them on the tablet of your heart."

The Bible has so much wisdom for us to use and apply in every circumstance. As we grow in our knowledge of Scripture, we can grow in our relationships. To do this, we have to read—and know—God's Word. We have to "write" verses on the tablets of our hearts.

You can walk around with an actual Bible like Christian and I do if you want to. But more importantly, I hope you'll go through each day with the transformational truths of God's Word walking around *inside you*. If you try to get by on your own understanding, your own wisdom, your own version of truth, you'll get yourself into trouble every time. But if you rely on what God says is wise and true, you can confidently move forward.

HOW TO PUT LOVE FIRST

The word of God is the most powerful thing we can carry around with us for security, confidence, and a reminder of who we are. I encourage you today to pick a verse to meditate on and memorize it! You will be amazed by how much impact that one verse you have planted in your heart will refresh your soul.

GOD HOLDS YOU STEADY

Blessed is the man who remains steadfast under trial, for when
he has stood the test he will receive the crown of life, which
God has promised to those who love him. JAMES 1:12

SADIE

GIVEN THE CIRCUMSTANCES OF HONEY'S BIRTH, SHE COULD
have come into the world with brain damage, a broken shoulder, and
severe trauma. I could have faced an emergency C-section and the real
possibility of bleeding out.

Thankfully those things didn't happen. But for way too long during that hospital stay, I firmly believed they would.

I realize this may be TMI, but for those who love a good birth
story, this is for you. During the final stages of delivery, Honey got
stuck in the birth canal. With a typical delivery, from the moment
a baby's head crowns, it takes three to five seconds for the rest of the
body to come out. It took Honey two minutes and ten seconds. Her
head made it out just fine, but then her birth stopped. Complicating
matters, the umbilical cord had wound its way around Honey's neck
before she entered the birth canal, and she couldn't breathe for more
than two minutes, which is an eternity in this situation.

The doctor later told Christian and me that if this had gone on
another twenty or thirty seconds, he would have had to literally push
the baby back inside my body and rush me into emergency surgery for
a C-section.

Back in the birthing room, with Honey partially born, the staff
realized the problem was shoulder dystocia, which requires the doctor
to break the baby's arm to be delivered.

Weeks before, Christian and I had put together a three-hour

playlist of the songs we wanted to hear during labor. It included one of our favorite songs, *Million Little Miracles*, which started playing right when Honey was born. Just as things were most desperate, I heard the downbeat of that song.

I was already crying, but now tears flowed for a different reason. When the lyrics started talking about living with an open heart, living like I know who God is, the doctor physically pushed on my abdomen to free Honey, leaving bruises that would take weeks to heal. In that moment, I let the vision of those lyrics wash over me. It's easy to live with an open heart when everything is awesome and beautiful and fun. But when the baby you're trying to deliver is crashing, you seriously wonder if you're going to live to tell about the day.

You've likely been in a situation where trouble surrounded you on every side. Where you felt completely alone, and nothing was going like it was supposed to.

How do we open our hearts to those days, too, to the days we wish would never happen?

Honey's first solo breath yielded the loudest cry as the song's title line rose: "Miracles on miracles . . . a million little miracles."

My nine-pound-five-ounce chunky miracle had arrived and was healthy.

I'm so glad for the outcome of that story, but we need to have that steadiness *before the resolution occurs*. It's easy to be calm after God has swooped in and made terrible things all right. What's not so easy is remaining steady in the midst of trauma, trusting that He will use *even this* for good. Steadiness is spiritual certainty in uncertain times.

HOW TO PUT LOVE FIRST

What are you stressed about today? What are you anxious about? Allow God's steadiness to rest over you right now before you see the resolution occur.

GOD MAKES YOU HIS

If we live by the Spirit, let us also keep in step
with the Spirit. GALATIANS 5:25

CHRISTIAN

NOT LONG AGO A GUY WHO WAS INTERVIEWING ME FOR HIS
podcast said, "Christian, you seem really content in life now that you're
a husband and a father. Just out of curiosity, do you ever miss being
single?"

The question caught me off guard because, in all honesty, I
can't remember the last time I thought about being single. I can't
remember the last time I thought about my life during my pre-Sadie,
pre-Honey days.

While it's true that I'm a total introvert who loves alone time,
quiet spaces, and smaller groups rather than large, I can't imagine my
life without my wife and child and the huge family I married into. I'd
never, ever want to go back.

There's a spiritual parallel here that I want to draw your attention
to. You could say that at this point in my life, I'm totally "in step"
with Sadie. We used to live separate lives, but once we were together,
everything became "ours." Her plans influenced my plans. My dreams
influenced her dreams. Her needs influenced my needs. My ideas
influenced her ideas. Her existence and my existence intertwined until
eventually there was just an "us."

And because I see how amazing and inspiring and life-giving that
"us" is, I never want to return to the time when it was just her life and
my life, apart from each other.

This is also what happens when we give our lives over to God.
His will influences our will. His ways affect our ways. His desires

transform our desires. His priorities dictate ours. Over time we become so wrapped up in God's interests that we can no longer discern our interests from His. Galatians 5:25 calls this process keeping "in step with the Spirit," which is imagery I love. I like picturing myself walking *so closely* with God that if He were to stop abruptly, I'd bump into Him.

> I like picturing myself walking *so closely* with God that if He were to stop abruptly, I'd bump into Him.

If you're in a season of life when God feels distant to you, the answer isn't to run back to the version of you that wasn't surrendered to God. The answer is to alter your pace so that you're completely in step with Him.

God is always near, even in the seasons when we feel distant from Him. I love the comfort that comes from knowing that when I am feeling far from God, it is my own doing, not His. It is easy to blame God when we feel like He isn't near, when in reality we are the ones who have been "too busy," been entangled with sin, or even been hesitant to come back to Him. He is always there, waiting for us to walk in step with Him. He doesn't rush us or slow us down—He just wants us to be with Him.

HOW TO PUT LOVE FIRST

Slow down today and embrace where God has you. There's an idea called the art of taking a two-minute vacation. Take two minutes out of your day to relax your mind.

GOD'S TREASURES ARE ETERNAL

"But lay up for yourselves treasure in heaven, where
neither moth nor rust destroys and where thieves
do not break in and steal." MATTHEW 6:20

SADIE

I WAS SEVENTEEN YEARS OLD WHEN I WENT ON THE REALITY
TV show *Dancing with the Stars*. Week after week, I would sit down
for interviews, and the producers would say, "Okay, we just need you to
talk about how much you want to win the Mirrorball." The Mirrorball
Trophy was the reward given to the winning couple, and essentially the
goal of the show was to win it.

One of my competitors had just been interviewed and said, "It has
always been my life's goal to win the Mirrorball." How was I supposed
to compete with that?

The truth was, I was just happy to be there. I had overcome my
nearly debilitating fear of getting on an airplane to travel a couple of
states away from home and agreed to give it a go. I'd already won just
by showing up and discovering I could actually dance! Cheesy, I know,
but that is the truth!

Now, contrast that with an award show Christian and I attended
last month. It was the K-LOVE Fan Awards, and *Whoa, That's Good*
was up for Podcast of the Year. I really wanted to win that award. It
mattered to me in a deeply personal way that the Mirrorball hadn't.
When the hosts called my name as the winner, I felt so overwhelmed.
I'd never pictured myself winning at an awards show! And to win it
for my podcast meant so much to me. When I reached the stage at the
Grand Ole Opry, I felt humbled. Overjoyed. Undone.

People from all over the world tell me what an impact my podcast has made on their lives. Girls have told me that they listen to my podcast every day before school to help them feel more confident in their faith. I wanted that K-LOVE trophy, not because of what it meant in terms of worldly accolades, but because I believe what I am doing matters and has a purpose.

Here's a funny aside to that night at the awards show: I was so excited to receive that trophy, but as soon as I walked backstage a member of the K-LOVE crew took it from my hands. "This one is just a prop," he explained, "but we'll send you a real one in the mail."

Easy come, easy go, right? You know what? It didn't matter at all. I realized that it wasn't even the trophy I was after. I was after *impact that comes from God*. I was after the joy of walking in obedience to the Lord and seeing the fruit that it produced.

When Jesus coached His followers on how to live life, He told them to "lay up for yourselves treasures in heaven, where neither moth nor rust destroys and where thieves do not break in and steal. For where your treasure is, there your heart will be also" (Matthew 6:20–21).

I watched the funeral of Queen Elizabeth, and it struck me that before they buried her casket, they took the crown off. The crown cannot go with her on past death. Even the queen's treasures are not eternal. Maybe generational, but not eternal. However, I believe she went on to get her eternal crown in heaven.

Rust can eat away at metal trophies and crowns, but it can't erode the life changes that come by the hand of God. Is that the reward you're hoping for today? It's the only reward that lasts.

HOW TO PUT LOVE FIRST

Spend some time today thinking about the one pursuit, thing, or person that has the majority of your attention right now. Is it storing up eternal reward for you? If not, release it to God. If so, thank Him and ask for His help in continuing to pursue eternal things.

GOD GIVES YOU HIS JOY

And do not be grieved, for the joy of the LORD
is your strength. NEHEMIAH 8:10

SADIE

SOME DAYS I STRUGGLE TO MAKE SENSE OF WORLD EVENTS
and the headlines that make the news. When I scroll through all my
feeds and take in all the hatred and violence and abuse that is so ram-
pant these days, I feel like I need a shower, like I
need to somehow scrub off the awfulness.

> Joy isn't some
> light, fluffy
> concession.
> Joy is a hard-
> won choice.

That's when I pick up my Bible. How do I seek
the joy of the Lord for my strength when the world
is falling apart?

I've sometimes heard people who are joyful
described as naïve or out of touch, but on the days I
sit with the world's pain, joy isn't some light, fluffy
concession. Joy is a hard-won choice.

There's a story in the Old Testament about a prophet named
Nehemiah, who was an Israelite and who loved being part of God's
chosen nation. When he received word that the wall surrounding the
city of Jerusalem had been destroyed and the gates had been burned
down by warring tribes, he returned to his homeland to help rebuild.

He told the people stories about God's greatness and pointed out
their sinfulness, which caused them to weep tears of sorrow, of contri-
tion, of determination to go God's way instead of their own. Nehemiah
and another priest named Ezra told the people, "Do not be grieved, for
the joy of the LORD is your strength" (Nehemiah 8:10).

Even in the midst of their city's desolation and the weight of their
sins, they could choose the joy of the Lord to be their strength.

Joy doesn't come from deleting our news apps and sticking our heads in the sand and pretending that nothing is wrong in the world . . . or in our hearts. Joy comes from facing the awfulness head-on while *remembering that God is over it all*. Joy comes from being rooted in the Word of God and anchored in the peace that He alone can provide. It comes from being sure that despite all the pain and suffering we see and experience, there is still so much to be joyful about: we have a Savior whose name is Jesus, and He has come to rescue us from our sin.

I know things can get depressing in life. People let us down. Friends betray us. Spouses make cutting remarks. Total strangers wound us online. On a larger scale, there are abuses and aggressions and shootings and violence that are ridiculously common now.

When life gets hard, you may not see joy in anything or anywhere. And that's okay. I'm not asking you to be fake or put on a happy face. But I know that there is a transcendent joy that comes only from God that has a way of breaking through, that holds us in our pain and weathers all storms. The joy of His strength is yours for the taking.

You can't fake it; you can't force it. But you can ask God for it. Today, ask God for His joy to be your strength.

HOW TO PUT LOVE FIRST

As you read the news and scroll through headlines today, mourn the sadness and give the pain to God. Then ask Him to give you His joy to be your strength. Ask Him to give that joy to those in pain.

GOD HAS GREAT PLANS FOR YOU

The heart of man plans his way, but the LORD
establishes his steps. PROVERBS 16:9

SADIE

I HAD LUNCH WITH A FRIEND WHO IS PASSIONATE ABOUT HER
future, and the conversation quickly turned to where she wanted to be
in ten years.

I was super-impressed that she had such clarity on what she
wanted to do in life. Most people our age aren't clear on what they
want to do in the next ten minutes, let alone the next ten years. They
don't know what the purpose of life is, and they don't know what their
purpose *within* life is. I even wrote about this concept in my previous
book, *Who Are You Following?*, and called it "purpose anxiety."

It's so common, but it doesn't have to be as hard as we sometimes
make it.

Scripture tells us that God made everything for a purpose—the
oceans, the trees, the sky, the animals, the bugs, and every human
being. He's a planner. He thinks ahead. He looks forward to what's to
come. And because you and I were made for a purpose, it's important
to seek that out.

Christian and I once went to Colorado to meet with a life coach—
someone who helps people figure out how God made them, what
dreams they have for the future, what gifts they can use in service to
others, and how to deal with obstacles that could get in their way. It
was an amazing time. It was also an *exhausting* time. Stepping back
and assessing why we're doing what we're doing often takes mental and
emotional energy we're not used to expending. It's tough to slow down
long enough to evaluate where we're going in life, but that's exactly
how we can be sure we're on the right track.

I encourage you to spend some time with these questions Christian and I talked through (for hours on end):

1. Which people in your life today do you want to stay invested in? (Our answers centered around our families, our local friends, our out-of-town friends, mentors, and teammates.)
2. What are you passionate about? (Christian loves fitness. I love speaking and events. We both love our podcasts. Well, and *Jesus*, of course.)
3. What spiritual gifts do you possess? (I'm a starter, an ideas person, a creator. Christian is more of a realistic, how-can-we-get-this-done type of guy. That is why we make a great team.)
4. How effectively are you using your gifts to honor God? (This one took some conversation to assess. I highly recommend investing whatever time you need.)
5. In ten years, if you were doing anything your heart desired, what would that thing be? (Christian is still mulling, but I would be hosting a talk show on TV, like Oprah. Hey, a girl can dream!)

At the end of the day we can sit here and plan all we want, but it's the *Lord* who establishes our steps. God has a purpose for you. If you don't know what it is yet, here's my advice: Dream. Dream *big*. Plan your heart out. And then grab hold of your heavenly Father's hand and step into the future anticipating great things from your great God.

HOW TO PUT LOVE FIRST

Today's challenge is in two parts. First, grab a journal and start praying over your dreams and the questions I presented. Write down every dream that comes to mind. Next, send an encouraging text to someone who's struggling to find purpose *or* someone who is hustling hard right now.

GOD IS GROWING SOMETHING IN YOU

"I am the vine; you are the branches. Whoever abides
in me and I in him, he it is that bears much fruit, for
apart from me you can do nothing." JOHN 15:5

SADIE

MY PARENTS HAVE BEEN TRYING TO START A GARDEN FOR
years, and recently they finally did it. They poured endless time and
energy into planning for it, clearing space in their front yard for it,
planting it, and tending it. And while my dad literally beams every
time he's able to include in his amazing dinnertime creations the
strawberries or tomatoes or potatoes he's picked from his very own
garden, he and my mom both would tell you that this gardening thing
is *hard*. To take a tiny little seed and turn it into a beautiful, ripe veg-
etable is *work*.

This is how it always is, for one thing to become another. Fruit (or
vegetables!) requires work. But we often want the fruit of labor without
doing the "labor" part at all.

We want the Insta-worthy, raised-bed garden and the pale-olive
gardening boots, the beautiful hats, and the wheelbarrow filled to
overflowing with all the amazing stuff we've grown. My mom started
out with the cute hat and the fun wheelbarrow, but when she realized
how much work was required, it wasn't quite so photo-worthy. It's hard
to want to be out there in the heat of the day, sweat dripping down our
faces, hands getting ripped up by weeds, bugs crawling up our sleeves.

But the truth is, we don't get the fruit of our labor without actually
doing the work. We don't get a harvest without tending the garden. It
takes work to make something new. It takes work to make something
good. It takes work to live life the way God has asked us to.

In the past year my entire family has faced some of the most challenging circumstances of our lives. Most days have not been picking strawberries for dinner. Most days have felt like being on our knees in the garden in the sweltering heat, picking thorny weeds one at a time.

But I've been getting the sense that if I just stay committed to God's calling on my life, if I just keep my hands in the dirt, He will turn those seeds of faithfulness into beautiful, sweet fruit. Last month I told Christian that the only thing I wanted for my upcoming birthday was a new Bible. I wanted the Bible so that I'd have a clean slate where I could record that process of growth, that process of transformation, that process of God doing something totally new in and through my life. He is growing me as a wife. He is growing me as a mom. He is growing me as a leader. He is growing me as a friend. I want to contribute to that work instead of stifling it. I want to *welcome* His life-giving ways.

And I want the same for you. If you're in a weed-picking phase right now, don't lose heart. God is growing something beautiful in that garden. He is miraculously turning seed into fruit, something only He can bring about. He is changing your life for good.

HOW TO PUT LOVE FIRST

If you have access to a garden, a plant, or anything that you take care of—your work, your child, your pet—take an extra meaningful moment today to nurture and care for it. As you do, thank God for the growth you've seen in your faith. Are there areas where He is pruning you now to grow even more?

GOD MAKES YOU PURE

The Lord God commanded the man, saying, "You may surely
eat of every tree of the garden, but of the tree of the knowledge
of good and evil you shall not eat." GENESIS 2:16-17

CHRISTIAN

SEVERAL MONTHS BEFORE SADIE AND I GOT MARRIED, WE
were in Florida to visit my parents. One afternoon, I happened to be
walking by the front door when I noticed a black snake on the front
porch. It was *giant*.

My parents had left to run an errand, so it was just Sadie and me
there. I knew she'd gone upstairs to take a shower, but when she heard
the urgency in my voice to come see what was outside, she came flying
down the stairs. We were both watching the snake's movement, freak-
ing out at how big it was, when I happened to glance over and discover
that my fiancée had nothing but a towel on.

Suddenly I wasn't so intrigued by the snake.

I'll say at the outset that Sadie and I did not have sex that day, but
this was a moment when we got sidetracked. When she and I started
dating, we studied God's Word, prayed a lot together, and then had a
serious conversation about what our physical boundaries would be. We
talked about how deeply we desired to see God's plan play out in our
lives, and that included a desire for purity.

But that day with the snake on the front porch, we briefly forgot
that conversation and pushed the boundaries.

In Genesis 2, we learn that God made man and placed him in
the garden. Then He told the man not to eat of a particular tree, and
if he did, he would die. You probably know how this story ends. God

created woman. The man told the woman the rule. And then both of them chose to defy God's orders and eat from the forbidden tree.

After Sadie and I realized what we were doing that afternoon in Florida, and what was about to happen if we didn't reverse course fast, we felt shame sweep over us, just like it did Adam and Eve. It was a horrible feeling.

At a Passion conference a few years ago, Pastor John Piper said that if we spend our lives trying to do the right thing and avoid the wrong thing, we will always, always fail. If instead we spend our lives trying to do the will of God, because we truly desire His will, then we will always make the right choice. It was really hard to make the right decision that day, but what helped us course-correct was knowing that God had something better for us. It was not our boundary talk that stopped us, but our desire for God's will.

If you and I trust that the heart of God is good and kind and merciful, that He is *for us* every day, then we won't fixate on following a set of commandments or restrictions or rules. We'll simply fix our eyes on *Him* to know that we're choosing well.

HOW TO PUT LOVE FIRST

It's far better for us to choose God's plan, to choose God's path, to let purity rule the day. Far better to run this race set before us as weightlessly as we possibly can. What do we need to lay down today to choose God's will rather than simply following a set of rules?

GOD MADE YOU UNIQUELY YOU

God created man in his own image . . . male and female he
created them. And God blessed them. GENESIS 1:27–28

SADIE

ONE DAY RECENTLY ON VACATION, I HAD AN INSECURE
thought. Shocking, right? A girl having an insecure thought while
wearing a bathing suit at the beach? Yeah, not so shocking at all. But
it got me thinking about how someday my sweet, innocent, adorable
daughter, Honey James, will also have insecure thoughts. And that
broke my heart. Honey isn't just any girl; she's *my* girl. And I see how
amazing she is.

People have always told me that once I had my own child, my
eyes would be opened to how thoroughly and completely I am loved by
God. That reality has absolutely played out. I see with fresh perspective how God sees me—as His amazing little girl.

God sees you that way too. If you could grasp how thoroughly and
completely God loves you, it would be hard to ever feel insecure. If
you've gained a few pounds or have a little more acne during those hot
summer days, I feel you. But the truth is that your worth isn't defined
by your looks, your job, or anything else. It's defined by your heavenly
Father, who, from the beginning, declared you *good*.

I already tell Honey all these things, even though she may not
understand a word just yet. I say to her, "Honey, you were made
wonderfully. As you grow up, I pray you never look to the right or the
left. I pray you just look to Jesus."

If I could sit across from you right now, I'd say the very same thing
to you: Don't look to the right or to the left. I mean, who are you trying
to copy? You're an original! Keep your eyes fixed on Jesus, the One who

died so that you can live. He is writing the sweeping saga that is the story of your life, and He never, ever makes mistakes. He created you on purpose for a purpose, and that purpose is unique to *you*. You're not lost in the crowd to Him. You're special. One of a kind.

I had a girl leave our Live Original team not long ago, and during her exit interview, she said, "I'll really miss being here, but I know there are a thousand people who can do what I was doing for you."

That is not true. Sure, I can find another person to step in and check off the actual tasks that she was tending to. But I'll never find someone just like her because she's the only *her* there is. I know this because I've watched people come and go since LO was first launched. And while I have filled open spots with very capable people, it doesn't change the fact that when someone leaves the team, they take something distinctive with them, the thing that is theirs, divinely, alone.

That's what originality is. It's the you-ness of who you are. Your dreams, your perspective, your attitude, your joy, your insights, your laughter, your vibe.

You're *good*. You're seen. You're valued. You're loved. You're *you*, with all the wonders and talents that includes. You're an original, never to be replicated again.

HOW TO PUT **LOVE** FIRST

I love dancing. However, I'm not the best dancer in the world—if you turn on music I may not do the trendiest moves. But you better believe I will bust a move. Christian is not a good dancer from the world's terms, but I love his dancing because they are his dance moves and make me laugh the hardest. What are your dance moves? What is it that brings out the confidence and joy in you?

GOD IS DEVOTED TO YOU

Now set your mind and heart to seek the LORD
your God. 1 CHRONICLES 22:19

CHRISTIAN

MY BROTHER PLAYS BASEBALL FOR A D1 COLLEGE, AND LIKE
all D1 schools, that program has some *fans*. They know every player
by number, position, year in school, hometown, and career stats. They
think about their baseball team. They talk about it. They spend an
insane amount of time and money supporting it. They are *devoted*, and
that devotion shows.

You might not be that into college baseball, but I bet if I talked to
you for five or ten minutes, I could find something you are really into.
I spend a lot of time interviewing people for my podcast, and I love to
learn what lights up my guests. Sometimes it's someone who loves to
travel—they can't help but smile as they tell me all about it. Sometimes
it's an author or a pastor or a musical group. Often it's someone with a
new workout approach or program, and it's like they can't get the words
out fast enough to tell me why it's so great.

I was thinking about this recently after talking to a guy who said,
"I can tell how much you love Jesus, Sadie, and Honey because every
story you tell seems to come back to one of those three."

We both laughed. I *do* love Honey and Sadie in ways that are
tough to describe. How weird would it be if I felt this way but never
expressed it in my words and actions? Would you truly believe I loved
them, that I was devoted to them?

There are a ton of things to be "into" in this life. The world is
an amazing place. People are fascinating. Sports are fun. Movies and
books give us glimpses into new aspects of life. But there's one thing

the most relationally healthy people I know are into, and that's Jesus Christ.

I love how that guy on my podcast mentioned Jesus first in the lineup of the three people I talk most about. There was a time in my life when that wasn't the case. I went through a long stretch when I was out for my own good instead of living surrendered to Jesus, and my relationships suffered a lot.

One decision changed everything for me—it helped me start to cultivate healthy and honest relationships in my life. That decision was to elevate my devotion to Jesus above everything else. It was to start thinking about Jesus more than I thought about anything else. It was to talk about Jesus more than I talked about anything else. It was to give time and energy and money to the cause of Jesus Christ instead of pouring it into habits and addictions that were taking me nowhere fast.

If you're sideways with your spouse, your parents, your kids, or a close friend today, and you don't know where to start, start where I did a few years ago, when I was at odds with pretty much the entire world: devote yourself to Jesus, and trust Him to guide you into wholeness and health, for yourself and for the people you love the most. God is utterly and completely devoted to you, and when you devote yourself to Him, you'll be amazed at how it impacts you and your relationships.

HOW TO PUT LOVE FIRST

Today, let's look at our calendars and see what our time is currently devoted to. What needs to change so we can be more fully devoted to God?

PAUSE AND REFLECT WITH DR. JOSH KIRBY

AS YOU COME TO THE END OF THE FIRST THIRTY DAYS OF this journey, and before you read on for the next thirty days, pause. Take a breath. Reflect on the Scriptures and what you have learned about God and your relationship with Him.

For most of us, we are quick to move into action. We feel a need to go, see, do, and attempt to control. In my practice, the people who come to me for my help often rush into my office from their busy lives, large coffee in hand, struggling to slow down and be present, even in a counseling session scheduled for them to do just that.

Instead of rushing to the next thing, let's pause. I believe you will be amazed by how spending small moments of purposeful attention will begin to shape your experiences hour to hour, day to day.

A DAILY PRACTICE

The more you can incorporate strategic pauses and moments of purposeful attention by connecting with God, your Creator, throughout your day—every day—the more you will see Him transforming your life and shaping your relationships. But you must be still, be present, and be in the moment in order to genuinely connect with your Father, God.

When we are unable to be present, to really see what is in front of us, we can begin to feel we are losing control. Our fear of being vulnerable takes over, and we continue rushing. It becomes even more difficult for us to settle into the supernatural presence of God. Begin each day by bringing awareness to your thoughts and feelings, whatever they are, and acknowledging them before Him. Bringing attention to our inevitably imperfect human experiences as we stand before our almighty God can help us live more freely in Him. A daily practice of slowing down and seeking God from this place of awareness will strengthen this most important relationship, which in turn will strengthen and impact all your other relationships.

> Bringing attention to our inevitably imperfect human experiences as we stand before our almighty God can help us live more freely in Him.

GOD'S PERFECTION AND OUR IMPERFECTION

Many of us grow up learning that God is perfect and all-powerful as well as relational and intimate. By the time we are old enough to sit still in Sunday School, we begin singing of God's perfect power. "There's *nothing* my God cannot do!" rings out from the tiny voices in kids' classrooms of churches everywhere. As we grow, though, many of us develop the awareness of our imperfection. Some may not be able to articulate the emptiness within or the sense of the vast difference between God's perfection and our imperfection, but we know we are not as we should be. We were created in His perfect image, and we strive to be perfect, too, even though we are flawed and broken.

In working with my clients over the years, I have noticed that many come to counseling already labeling themselves as perfectionists as they are seeking help in feeling burdened by their own unrealistic expectations. They are often exhausted by a sense of incongruence in their lives. For some, I believe it can be helpful to give a name to the patterns of behavior they want to change. I also believe this trend communicates something about all of us. Whether you personally relate to a label of perfectionism or not, we all have an understanding that perfection is not a human reality. Yet, most of us at some point in our lives will find ourselves in a cycle of making mistakes and then feeling miserably disappointed, as though perfection was always the goal. Two steps forward, three steps back is how my clients might describe it as they work week to week toward progress.

When we get stuck in life and feel we are not making progress, we may even begin to compare our efforts and results with those of others or the unrealistic expectations that have formed within us. That can breed fear in us—fear that we will not be enough, or we will not receive approval or love if we fail to meet the highest standards. "I made a mistake" becomes "I'm a failure." Attempting to make sense of who we are in the tension between our imperfection and God's perfection can lead us to lose temporary perspective of our eternal purpose.

But perfection is never the ultimate goal. God alone is perfect, and when we can accept our imperfection in light of God's perfection, we can truly be transformed through our relationship with Him. All of our striving, fear, anxiety, and imperfections are covered by His perfect love and grace. It is in our dependency on Him alone that provides our lasting perspective and purpose.

LIVING COVERED BY HIS PERFECT LOVE AND GRACE

When my oldest son was born, I gained a completely new comprehension of both the all-encompassing power of God's love *and* the psychological theory of human attachment. I have written about, spoken about, and helped many people in counseling using my education and training in this science of human bonding and relationships. I have spent many hours examining my own attachment origins through professional counseling; yet, in a single first breath, what had taken years to research and develop took on a new significance. Holding my newborn son in my hands taught me more about the significance of dependency and vulnerability than any textbook, classroom lecture, or clinical experience had ever done.

From the moment the nurse handed me my son, I realized that this beautiful baby boy's life was literally, now, in my hands. Newborns teach us that humans are dependent, from day one, on relationship. And though caregivers provide for physical and bodily needs, more importantly, they provide for our relational needs. Our longing for connection was created from and in God's image. So is our longing for connection with others. He placed these needs, these desires, within all of us. We are relational beings, created by a relational God whose own nature is a relationship: the Trinity, made up of Father, Son, and Holy Spirit.

As we grow and become more complex human beings, our relationships become more complex. We rely on family and trusted friends to delight in us, provide safety and care, hold us steady, and help us repair mistakes and redeem our failures. Yet, no human relationship is perfect, of course. We are all touched by sin and error, and that affects even our closest and best connections, leading to moments of misattunement and mistrust. When ruptures in relationships occur, we can feel tension and vulnerability, and we may even become emotionally cut off or try to self-protect. To avoid further disconnection, we might behave in ways that may not ultimately be helpful but temporarily serve our needs. But there is hope for all relationships. For Christians, our ultimate hope is in our connection with God. He is never misattuned to our needs. His relational nature is perfect in all ways, and we are free to be completely dependent on Him in all things.

GOD TRANSFORMS US AND OUR RELATIONSHIPS
God is a perfect parent, a good Father, and always near, even when we do not sense it. Our need for attachment is met in Him. His story, His commands, His desires, and His wisdom are available to you at any time through His Word. If you are in a moment or season of doubt, comparison, or shame, ask God to speak to you through Scripture

> When you
> faithfully allow
> God to lead
> you through
> spiritual
> disciplines, you
> will find that He
> will create room
> in your heart
> for connection
> with Him.

and prayerful meditation as you imagine He would speak to someone you care for. When you faithfully allow God to lead you through spiritual disciplines, you will find that He will create room in your heart—room perhaps you didn't even know you had left—for connection with Him. It is in this space deep within you that you will begin to feel most seen, fulfilled, and at peace.

Our bodies, our minds, and our emotions were created by God to carry us through this earthly life in connection and communication with Him. Many of us have learned to defend ourselves against pain and hurt, to turn our thoughts and emotions off, to judge ourselves for having them, or to dangerously indulge them. Past crises, struggles, and difficulties in relationships often shape these defenses that can become deeply internalized over time when we fail to maintain self-awareness.

In therapy, it is essential that I help my clients become aware of what their internal world, their senses, their minds, and their emotions are telling them. For one, it allows them to slow down the urge either to suppress or to react to what they are feeling. As they are able to regulate their feelings, we begin to focus on clarifying and rewriting the narratives that come out of those negative places. As they pay attention to their experiences within, they can turn to God who accepts us all, joyfully, fully. Even in their weaknesses, their nervous systems begin to be soothed, and they become increasingly attuned to the discernment of the Holy Spirit.

In your daily practice, as you notice what you are thinking and feeling, try to identify any hurt from the past, judgmental thoughts, anxiousness, discomfort, or urges that distract from what you are experiencing. Write these down throughout your week. You may notice recurring patterns that occur outside of your full awareness. Once you have written these down, I encourage you to go to Scripture and prayer, then write out a statement of God's truth that speaks to where you are in your week. Bring your attention to our God that is with you always, inviting Him to join you in that place.

Our God is always faithful and always attends to us intimately like only He can. This was Jesus' mission coming to earth as a human being. He was born into a human body, to feel what we feel, endure what we endure, and die for each and every one of us. He knew the innermost parts of every person He encountered and treated them according to how He made them—in His image, original, with a unique purpose—providing hope in ways only He knew they needed. This is how He sees you in your life today.

> **Our God is always faithful and always attends to us intimately like only He can.**

Maturing in Jesus is a lifelong process that most of us do by dying to ourselves, growing, regrowing, and dying again. As humans, we are not consistent. Jesus is always consistent in His love and grace. He sees us as beloved, adopted, and uniquely known sons and daughters of God. The more we learn to accept this from Jesus, the more we can begin to accept this for others. This is the foundation for all spiritually healthy relationships and for our community of faith. When we learn to put His love first, it opens us up to the joy of connection with others in their imperfections and our own.

Before you begin the next thirty days, take another moment to pause. I often suggest to my clients at the end of a session that they sit in their car in silence for a few minutes to transition well back into the busyness of their day. Give yourself permission to do that now, asking God to speak through Sadie and Christian's thoughts on placing love first in our closest relationships.

PART 2

YOUR RELATIONSHIP WITH YOUR PEOPLE

MOVING PAST YOUR PAST

Therefore, confess your sins to one another and pray for one another, that you may be healed. The prayer of a righteous person has great power as it is working. JAMES 5:16

SADIE

DURING A SEASON WHEN BOTH A LOT OF NEW THINGS WERE coming together in my life and I was having trouble getting past my past, I had an interesting dream. In the dream, I was in the White House walking along a massive corridor toward a room where I was to meet with the president of the United States.

Big day, right? It would have been, if only I'd been able to focus on the incredible moment at hand. But I couldn't because I kept getting distracted by everything I was seeing en route.

All along that hallway were doors leading into rooms, and every time I passed one of those rooms, I noticed that the door was wide open. I could see *everything* inside—and it was all stuff I didn't want to see: my past fumbles, past failures, past opportunities I'd squandered, past sin, past people.

As I made my way down the hall, I became increasingly burdened by everything from my past and increasingly resolved that I had no good reason to be in that stately mansion and no good reason to meet the president.

I made it to the meeting room, where the president awaited my arrival, but I was so broken down over the emotional baggage I carried that instead of approaching *the president*, I threw myself under the table and hid.

And then I woke up.

The next day, I told a good friend all about my dream, and she said, "You need to go close those doors. God's trying to bring you somewhere, but you can't go there until you let go of the stuff from your past."

I knew she was right, even as I didn't want her words to be true—because to "close those doors" meant I'd have to own my mistakes, and I'd have to make things right with the people I'd hurt. I'd have to have conversations I wasn't all that excited about having and offer apologies I felt embarrassed to extend.

And yet how else could I get past my past?

While I tried to make the wrong things right, I lived in a strange space. It was a pretty awkward time. But in the same way that a messy house isn't going to get transformed unless you clean it, my relationships were going to stay a mess until I started tidying, room by room.

If you're in this place of feeling imprisoned by your past, maybe some tidying is a good plan for you too. Where do you begin? *Acknowledge your part in the pain.* With a humble heart, go to the one you hurt. You were hurt too? Yep, I get that. But for now, own your part, say your piece, wish them well, and be on your way. And get busy doing what God wants you to do.

HOW TO PUT LOVE FIRST

What better way to start our relationship journey than owning our pasts and making amends where needed. Is there someone you need to reach out to today? Make a plan to do that and then pray that God will help you.

LETTING GOD FIGHT FOR YOU

The LORD will fight for you, and you have
only to be silent. EXODUS 14:14

CHRISTIAN

RECENTLY, SADIE AND I GOT INTO A MINOR TIFF BECAUSE,
evidently, I had had a bad tone all day long. We'd been running errands
and catching a movie, and when we got in the car afterward, I asked
her a simple logistical question and got a sassy comment in reply. I
mentioned the sassiness, and she lit up—and not in the good way.
We're talking dangerous sparks.

"You've got a problem with *my* tone now?" she said. "What about
the tone *you've* had all day long?"

Well, now we had a *thing*.

In the book of Ephesians, Paul told us to "be kind to one another,
tenderhearted, forgiving one another, as God in Christ forgave you"
(4:32). This is the concluding verse in the chapter, and it is also the last
verse under the subheading "The New Life" in my ESV Bible. This is
profound to me because before I knew Jesus, I was not walking in this
"newness of life" that the Bible so often talks about.

Without Jesus, I am not naturally kind or tenderhearted or even
quick to forgive others, but because He has imparted all of these attri-
butes to me, I can embrace them.

When Sadie was rude to me that day, my initial reaction and
instinct was not to be kind or extend tenderness. It was to be rude
and get defensive. It can be hard to change old habits and instinctive
reactions.

Sadie and I talk a lot about what makes a marriage work—or what
makes any intimate relationship work, for that matter. One theme we

keep coming back to is this: while we may argue from time to time, in the end we need to fight *for* each other, not against each other. And when that's hard for us to do, we find that if we are willing to ask for God's help and be silent before Him, He will go before us, soften our hearts, and fight the battles with us. We're committed to seeing each other through to becoming the people God wants us to be.

Hours after our little "tone discussion," Sadie and I put Honey to bed and then sat down on the couch to talk. God helped us each own our part of the day:

"I was tired all day and took it out on you," I said.

"I was fed up with your mood and just snapped," she said.

I'm sorry.

Will you forgive me?

We are *better than this.*

There's something a lot like Jesus going on in us when we fight for, not against, each other. Even when I'm in a bad mood, when I am hurtful to Him, He is committed to loving me and quick to forgive. He is always on my side. He is always for me. And He fights for both me and my relationships.

It's easy to get mad. But life is so much sweeter when we let God do our fighting. Today, when we get mad, let's take a deep breath and say a prayer before we respond.

HOW TO PUT LOVE FIRST

Who is the person in your life you are most likely to take a "tone" with? Do something extra sweet and kind for that person today. If you're currently having a moment, apologize for your part and offer better understanding as to where your tone is coming from. If not, give a hug, a text, a coffee—something—that says, I see you, I love you, and you matter to me.

GIVING AND RECEIVING HELP

What you have heard from me in the presence of
many witnesses entrust to faithful men, who will
be able to teach others also. 2 TIMOTHY 2:2

SADIE

JUST OUTSIDE THE RECORDING STUDIO WHERE I DO MY POD-
cast interviews is a board on the wall with notes all over it—the
amazing input I get week after week from guests of the *Whoa, That's
Good* show. If you've ever listened in, you know that my favorite question to ask people is "What's the best piece of advice you've ever been
given?" This board is filled with listener responses to that question,
and the answers always blow me away.

I've been following Jesus for more than half my life, but I'm still
getting discipled every day—including by my podcast guests. Some
people think of discipleship as a faith stage that only new believers go
through, but I believe we all have blind spots and areas where we need
to grow. We all need help on this journey called life. With that said, I
want to ask you two questions:

First, *who is helping you?* Do you have people in your life who are
wiser and more spiritually mature than you, maybe a little older than
you, to help you navigate the tough parts of life? Christian and I are
intentional about meeting up with mentors as often as we can, and the
wisdom they share with us is so valuable. If you don't have anyone who
is further along in their faith journey to speak into your life, ask God
to direct you toward that person or couple who might be able to help.
Also consider whether you talk honestly to your friends about the hard
stuff you are going through. Odds are, they can probably relate and are

eager to be there for you. Whatever you do, just start. We all need help, and we all need people to disciple us—at every season of life.

And then, secondly, *who are you helping?* I've always loved the passage of Scripture we call the Great Commission. It's basically the instructions Jesus left for His followers, right before He returned to heaven after coming to earth. "All authority in heaven and on earth has been given to me. Therefore go and make disciples of all nations, baptizing them in the name of the Father and of the Son and of the Holy Spirit, and teaching them to obey everything I have commanded you. And surely I am with you always, to the very end of the age" (Matthew 28:18–20 NIV).

God wants us to help others, to make disciples of all nations. He includes us in this Great Commission, to be a part of His mission on earth. He helps us see that the most loving thing we could do for another person is to tell them about Jesus' love and how to secure eternal life.

Are you being helped on your journey by someone who has walked closely with Jesus for longer than you? And are you purposefully helping someone else grow in their understanding of just how important a relationship with Jesus is?

HOW TO PUT **LOVE** FIRST

Pray about reaching out to someone who will mentor you and to someone for you to mentor. Who do you know who is wise, loving, and steady in their relationship with Jesus? Who do you know who might benefit from your life lessons? Invite someone to lunch and see what God does.

DAY 34

WINNING IN YOUR RELATIONSHIPS

But thanks be to God, who gives us the victory through
our Lord Jesus Christ. 1 CORINTHIANS 15:57

CHRISTIAN

I'VE BEEN AN ATHLETE MY WHOLE LIFE, AND ONE OF THE
things I love about sports is that it's always clear who's winning and
who's not. I'm a super-competitive person, so the worst thing someone
could say is "Hey, we don't need to keep score. Let's just play for fun."

That will never work for me. I like to win. And yet, while I'm all
about keeping score on the basketball court, the tennis court, and the
flag football field, there's one place I hope I never, ever keep score: in
the relationships God has placed in my life.

Can you imagine what kind of marriage Sadie and I would have if
I came up to her and said, "Hey, babe, I changed Honey's diaper, took
out the trash, and got the oil changed in both cars, so I'm at four points
so far today. Well, five, if you count the fact that I was a *little* more
patient than you were during the 'discussion' we had after breakfast.
Where you at?"

First of all, I'd never win in that game. Her list would be a
country-mile long. And second, why would I even want to play? Why
would *she*? We would be both winning and losing simultaneously,
which sounds awful.

What about in our relationship with God? What if we came with
a list of accomplishments at the end of each day and said, "So, God,
I kept my cool when I wanted to road-rage the dude who flipped me
off; I only struggled with regrets from my past four times today versus
yesterday's six; and overall I think my performance rates somewhere in
the nineties. What are we thinking for the reward here?"

It seems ludicrous, and yet we do it all the time. We don't get the promotion we wanted or the opportunity we were hoping for and reflexively blame God. We look around at other people who are *clearly* less spiritual than we are and throw an accusation heaven's way: "God, I tithe! I serve! I pray and read my Bible, and now *he* gets all the props?"

Whenever I'm tempted to twist the gospel of Jesus Christ into some sort of prosperity gospel, I remind myself that none of the disciples who followed Jesus in the first century looked like they were winning. They were marginalized, ostracized, persecuted, falsely accused, imprisoned, stoned, whipped, tormented, and, in some cases, crucified—all for following Jesus. Had there been a scoreboard posted somewhere in first-century Jerusalem, it would have read Romans: 8,347,281,902; Jesus followers: 0.

Sadie says it's a dangerous thing when we keep score with God. She's absolutely right because God has already won! He has conquered death, a clear and eternal victory.

"Thanks be to God, who gives us the victory through our Lord Jesus Christ" (1 Corinthians 15:57). No more keeping score—ever. From a kingdom perspective, it's just win after win after win after win after win.

ᕼᑗᗯ ᖶᑌ ᑭᑌᖶ **LOVE** ᖴᓮᖇᔕᖶ

Have you been keeping score with anyone lately? God or someone you love—or even someone you find rather hard to love? It's a trap most of us fall into at some point or another. Today, ask for God to give you clarity and strength to let it go and enjoy His wins.

DAY 35

EMBRACING PEACE

"Peace I leave with you; my peace I give to you. Not as the world gives do I give to you. Let not your hearts be troubled, neither let them be afraid." JOHN 14:27

SADIE

BEFORE I MET CHRISTIAN, I WAS IN A SERIOUS DATING relationship that was headed for marriage. I was eighteen, which seems very young to me now, but I thought we were in love, and he was just about to talk to my dad before asking me to marry him. Everything looked great from the outside, but on the inside I was a wreck.

I grew up in a family that had its fair share of tough times before I was even born. If people only know the TV show version of our story, it's easy to think things were always hilariously sweet. But they certainly weren't for my dad's family. Years before we ever had a TV show, there were all sorts of things going on in my extended family—addictions, dysfunctions, and even abuse. With all the misbehavior that occurred, it's a miracle my grandparents, aunts, and uncles are still married. I learned from watching them overcome so many obstacles that you had to fight for your marriage. You had to look past everything else and just *decide* to make it work.

I knew that my relationship with this boyfriend was hard. We fought all the time. I was constantly a stress case when he was around. But we were in love, right? We were going to get married soon. I just needed to get in there and *fight*.

Around that time, I met with a family friend who was a pastor, and she asked me, "Sadie, when you think about your relationship with this young man, do you feel at peace?"

The question caught me off guard. Peace? What did *peace* have to do with anything? I was gearing up for a *fight*.

She told me that while life wouldn't always be easy, when Jesus is in something, there is peace. "One of the fruits of the Holy Spirit is peace," she said. "When you're letting the Spirit lead you, you will experience and know peace."

When Jesus was preparing to go back to heaven, He pulled His followers together and told them He was leaving them with a gift. "Peace I leave with you; my peace I give to you," He said (John 14:27). Evidently that peace was mine for the taking.

I broke up with my boyfriend shortly after that because I realized I had forgotten what peace even felt like. I had cried a lot when we were dating because of the constant fighting. But after we broke up, I went about a year without being able to form any tears. That is, until Jesus softened my heart, and suddenly tears rolled down my cheeks. God began to show me what it felt like to be at ease in my skin, in my life, and in the world. He was helping me experience His peace.

God's peace feels like quiet tenderness, like a gentle reminder that you have nothing to prove, and like calm amid the world's chaos. It feels like ease.

Once I knew what God's peace felt like, I was able to have peace in my other relationships. And when I met Christian and we decided to get married? There was peace every step of the way.

HOW TO PUT **LOVE** FIRST

Do you have peace in your relationships, the kind that comes from God? What relationships in your life could use more of that peace? Are there some relationships you might need to prayerfully exit?

HAVING PATIENCE

I therefore, a prisoner for the Lord, urge you to walk in a manner worthy of the calling to which you have been called, with all humility and gentleness, with patience, bearing with one another in love. EPHESIANS 4:1-2

CHRISTIAN

WHEN HONEY WAS JUST DAYS OLD, SHE FELL INTO A PAT-tern that drove me crazy. She would wake up in the morning, get a fresh diaper, some milk, some cuddles. And then she'd cry. We would rock her, and eventually she'd settle down. But the moment we stopped rocking, she'd scream. It turned out she had colic.

To make matters worse, her version of colic came with an added bonus: projectile vomiting. Something like fifteen times a day, Honey would spit up every drop of milk she'd just ingested.

This went on for four months—that's sixteen weeks, which is also 112 days. I counted. I thought Honey and I both might cry every day for the rest of our lives.

I've never considered myself a patient person. I like efficiency. I like effectiveness. I like things to go according to plan. Sadie tells me that on day four or five of Honey's life, during a colicky episode, I leaned over the edge of Honey's bassinet and said, "You need to stop crying." I told her this, like she was actually old enough to understand—forgetting I was talking to a five-day-old baby!

I don't remember any part of that scene. I was so sleep deprived that I must have blocked it out totally. I can only describe what began to happen in my heart as a divine work of God. I realized that as a newborn baby, Honey relied on Sadie and me for *everything*: protection, comfort, food, kindness, cleanliness, stability, the whole deal. I started looking at Honey with tenderness instead of annoyance, with understanding instead of frustration. I'd be holding her while she screamed herself sweaty and red, and I'd think, *I'm responsible for this person. She's looking to me to help her here, to make things better, not worse.*

I started to see Honey's episodes as opportunities to practice patience and to be connected to God, to hold her and love her in the way He holds and loves us. I asked Him to tell me what "patient" would look and sound like each morning and again each night. I pleaded with Him to empower me to fight for a patient spirit so I could love Sadie and Honey well.

I'm not going to paint a sunny picture here: when it was three in the morning and Sadie was spent and Honey was still wailing, it wasn't like I was skipping throughout the house. It *stunk*. I was not happy about it. I was more exhausted than I knew was possible. But after a beat of despair, God's Spirit would prompt me to pray those same prayers again. And the more I desired for patience to emerge, the more patient I became. This is why character traits like patience are called the "fruit of the Spirit" in Galatians 5:22—because when we let the Holy Spirit have His way in our lives, the fruit of His presence starts to shine through our lives and our relationships.

HOW TO PUT **LOVE** FIRST

If you're struggling to practice patience, ask God to meet you in your moment of frustration; ask Him to help you see the person who is annoying you or causing you to struggle as someone who is hoping you'll show up for them, someone who might need some compassion, love, and patience.

SHOWING KINDNESS

Be kind to one another, tenderhearted, forgiving one
another, as God in Christ forgave you. EPHESIANS 4:32

SADIE

WHEN CHRISTIAN PICKED ME UP FOR OUR FIRST DATE, I
settled into the passenger seat and immediately noticed a new pack of
watermelon-flavored gum perched on the console. I laughed out loud,
stunned that he'd remembered.

We had met a few months before in Seaside, Florida, when we
were both on summer vacations with friends and family. We had gotten each other's numbers, and after DMing for a couple of weeks, we
began to talk on the phone all the time. During one of those calls,
I must have mentioned that I loved watermelon gum. It was such a
casual thing, I don't even remember saying it. But there it was on our
first date: proof that he'd paid attention, that he cared. Even though it
was such a small thing, he had noted it and wanted to make me smile.

After that, every time he picked me up for a date, a small surprise
was in the car waiting for me. I knew one thing without a doubt:
Christian Huff was *kind*.

Kindness is intentionally acting in the interest of another person,
and it has such impact. When Christian is kind, in big ways or small,
he shows me he loves me. And whenever we are kind to others, we
show people the heart of God, that He loves them. God's nature is to
be kind—He's always thinking of us, He pays attention, and He wants
us to delight in Him. And the impact of that is *eternal*.

When the apostle Paul was giving the believers in Ephesus
instructions on how to live out their faith, he closed his remarks with a
call for kindness: "Be kind to one another, tenderhearted, forgiving one

another, as God in Christ forgave you" (Ephesians 4:32). Paul knew that how the believers treated one another reflected the character of God, that their actions and words were a way to display God's kindness to them.

My great-grandmother, Mamaw Jo, likes to say, "You aren't kind because someone is kind to you; you're kind because you are a kind person. Kindness is who you are." Kindness shouldn't just be a reaction we have when others are kind to us. Rather, it should be a part of who we are, who God is making us into.

It's also a choice—one that we decide to live in and act on daily. I want to be kinder tomorrow than I am today. I want to increasingly act in the interest of others. I want to serve them by seeing them as God's.

Another Mamaw Jo-ism that's worth taking with you in life is this: "Nothing is worth harming another person to get." That's gold, right there. Just imagine how different our world would be if even a *fraction* of us lived by that rule! Disunity would decrease. Hatred and violence would decrease. And it would all be traced back to something as seemingly insignificant as *kindness*—that quiet, unassuming trait.

If this is an area where you need to grow, know that there are so many simple ways to be kind.

And if all else fails, start by buying a few packs of watermelon gum.

HOW TO PUT **LOVE** FIRST

Today, open the door for someone. Pay someone's tab at a restaurant or coffee shop. Give a loved one not just a passing "Hey" but a heartfelt, extended "How are you really doing?" Send a text of unexpected gratitude. Stop and ask a meaningful question.

GAINING SELF-CONTROL

A man without self-control is like a city broken into
and left without walls. PROVERBS 25:28

SADIE

MY HUSBAND IS GREAT AT TENNIS, WHICH IS A GOOD THING
because I love playing tennis. Christian is also great at basketball,
pickleball, baseball, bowling—you name it—and so when we were
dating and all throughout our engagement, we'd challenge various
friends and family members to a game and then unceremoniously kick
their booties. For the first eighteen months of our relationship, we
never lost a single game in any sport that we played together. We
were *on fire.*

Given how competitive Christian and I both are, you'd think this
season would have been our glory days. Let me tell you why it wasn't
so great after all.

One day my brother John Luke, who rarely plays tennis, and my
grandmother showed up on the tennis court and asked if we wanted to
play. Yes, you read that right—my *grandmother.* Before we could even
say yes, both of them started trash-talking us: "Oh, y'all think you're
so good, don't you? Y'all think nobody can beat you." And of course,
like any brother, John Luke knew just what to say to get in my head.

I was mad. Like, *really* mad.

The entire time we played, I was in my head, and tennis is a
very mental sport. I couldn't hit a shot to save my life, and Christian
couldn't get it together either. Before we knew it, we were pointing
our anger toward each other. We started accusing each other of not
playing hard enough, blaming each other for missed shots, harassing
each other just because we needed a target. It was awful.

Do I even have to tell you that we lost? This was three, almost four, years ago, and those two *still* bring up their win.

Christian and I laugh about the whole thing now, and I know it was just a silly tennis match, but what stunned me was my lack of self-control.

I once heard it said that self-control is the ultimate sign of a spiritually mature person because if you can master self-control—yielding to the Holy Spirit in stressful situations so He can manifest self-control in and through you—then all the other fruits, such as love and joy and patience and peace, will naturally flow from there. If I'd practiced self-control on the tennis court that day, I wouldn't have yelled at the love of my life for losing a tennis match. I wouldn't have let anger rule my thoughts. I wouldn't have been so hard on myself, and I would have had a *lot* more fun.

Self-control can be one of the hardest things to practice, but it's one of the most rewarding too.

My advice to you is to determine ahead of time—before a potentially stressful situation—to do everything you can to keep your cool. Pause and ask God to guard your heart and your mouth. Remember who you are. Remember *whose* you are.

HOW TO PUT LOVE FIRST

We all have triggers. It could be sports. Political conversations. That super-annoying thing your spouse does that drives you crazy. Let's identify our triggers and then pray for self-control. And today, let's make a plan to give God space to grow our self-control in those areas.

EXPERIENCING GROWTH

Grow in the grace and knowledge of our Lord
and Savior Jesus Christ. 2 PETER 3:18

CHRISTIAN

A FEW WEEKS AGO I HUNG OUT WITH MY COUSIN FOR THE
first time in a while, and even though he follows me on social media,
seeing me in person was a totally different thing. I'd been working
out a ton, and the minute he saw me, he was floored. "You're huge!"
he said, which made me laugh. "I'm *strong*," I replied, as I gave him a
quick bro hug.

It's always an ego boost to have someone notice the kind of growth
you get from being in a gym, but even better is noticeable growth in
your spiritual life.

About six months ago, I was scheduled to go on a men's retreat
with Sadie's dad, Willie. At the last minute, I had to back out because
of a scheduling conflict. So I reached out to my brother-in-law, Jacob,
to see if he wanted my spot.

I saw Jacob just before he went on that trip, and a day or two after
he got back, and I'm telling you: he wasn't the same guy. He had fallen
more in love with God. He had grown a massive amount spiritually.
And it showed. To this day, he points to that weekend retreat as a pivotal time in his life spiritually. To those on the sidelines, it was *obvious*
that this was the case. Jacob had encountered a deeper side of faith at
that retreat.

Sometimes spiritual growth doesn't hit us in a flash like that.
Sometimes it takes time. I think about my daughter, Honey, and how
she's clearly getting bigger every moment of the day. Sadie and I can't
really detect it until she outgrows a piece of clothing or fits differently

in our arms. That's how it can be for us in our relationship with Jesus too—the growth happens so subtly that it's barely perceptible to us. But over time, we ought to be able to detect that growth. We should be different than we were before.

When Sadie and I take Honey on a trip and get back a week later, our parents and siblings always go nuts over how big she has gotten. Her hair is longer. She has more words to say. She takes twenty steps on her own instead of five. On and on it goes. The same should be true for us. When we haven't seen a friend or family member in a while, our presence should reflect godly growth in our lives.

"You seem more at peace these days . . ."

"You're a lot more patient than you were before . . ."

"You were never this encouraging before . . . what's changed?"

The author of Hebrews tells us: "Therefore let us move beyond the elementary teachings about Christ and be taken forward to maturity, not laying again the foundation of repentance from acts that lead to death, and of faith in God" (Hebrews 6:1 NIV). Just like in life, once you move beyond elementary teachings in the classroom, people begin to notice a growth in the way you learn and act.

HOW TO PUT LOVE FIRST

People notice when you grow. In what ways are you actively striving to grow spiritually that will bless the people around you?

DAY 40
TAKING RESPONSIBILITY

Unless the LORD builds the house, those who
build it labor in vain. PSALM 127:1

CHRISTIAN

BY THE TIME SADIE AND I BROKE GROUND ON OUR HOUSE,
we had been planning for twenty months. After many setbacks and a
lot of changes and shifts in our life, we were finally ready to go. My
dad is in construction, and he helped us look over blueprints that his
architect drew up. We weighed options about putting an extra bed-
room in and about moving a bathroom around.

On some days, I'd feel pressure to make decisions, to do what
I could so it wouldn't take any longer than necessary. But then I'd
remember that Sadie and I want this house to be our forever home, a
warm and welcoming place where friends can relax for years to come.
We built super close to her family so that we could be near them for a
long time. We want our house to accommodate our family today and
the family God entrusts to us ten, twenty, thirty years from now.

During the building process, so many people told me horror stories about what it was like to build a home. They'd tell me how they
flew through the process and only later realized that they hated the
door handles or that their yard flooded whenever it rained or that the
exposed beams in the living room they were so excited about were
installed unevenly spaced.

I'm generally a quick decision maker who likes to get things done,
but on this important project, I realized I'd have to take my time and
pay attention to the details.

And so I'd drive by the house unannounced. I'd touch base with
the general contractor to see what was working and what was holding

things up. I'd ask questions and offer encouragement. I'd walk all over the property and pray. I considered this homebuilding process a big responsibility.

I like to think about the word *responsibility* as literally the ability to respond, the ability to see the truth of a given situation and react in an appropriate way. It's keeping a finger on the pulse of reality and doing what needs to be done. It's a critical skill in homebuilding and in the building of our relationships as well.

Throughout the building process, I thought about how easy it is to neglect some of my relationships. Some friendships have a daily rhythm where we drop each other a text or two every single day. Some have a weekly rhythm—I catch them at the gym, at a local restaurant, at church. Others are on an every-six-months basis, which means that a couple of times a year either they reach out to me or I give them a call. If I'm not careful to learn and honor the rhythm of each relationship, I risk losing the connection altogether. These relationships, especially the close ones, matter to me, and so I take them seriously and am responsible for their continual care.

I know it's easy to sit back and wait for the other person to initiate, but I figure that if I'm *able* to respond, then I will *choose* to respond. I'll be as responsible as I know how to—checking in with God and the people I do life with whenever I can.

HOW TO PUT LOVE FIRST

Who needs to hear from you today? Let's pause and send some messages to let people know they are loved, thought of, and cared for.

OFFERING FORGIVENESS

Then Peter came up and said to him, "Lord, how often will my brother sin against me, and I forgive him? As many as seven times?" Jesus said to him, "I do not say to you seven times, but seventy-seven times." MATTHEW 18:21–22

SADIE

SEVERAL YEARS AGO I POURED MY HEART AND SOUL INTO A friend. We did everything together. We went everywhere together. We were knitted together in that amazing way that best friends are, and I really thought I was the luckiest girl in the world to have a friendship like that.

I had started talking to this guy; however, I realized early on our connection wasn't strong enough to pursue anything. When I explained that I thought we should go our separate ways, he criticized me and was extremely rude. In a burst of frustration and spite he said, "I'm not going to carry you around on a pedestal like all your friends do. I'm not going to give you everything you want."

I'd only been talking to this guy for two weeks. How in the world had he so quickly come to these assumptions about me? As I tried to make sense of what he was saying, he blurted out my friend's name and said she was the one who told him "the truth" about me.

His words shocked my mind and broke my heart. It made me second-guess who I was and what people thought of me.

Over the days that followed, I learned that this friend had shared her bad opinion of me to our entire friend group behind my back. I went to her directly, and she admitted this. "I don't know why I did it, Sadie. I think I was just hurting from my own stuff and didn't know what to do."

I was heartbroken.

Later, she wrote me a long letter, explaining how sorry she was for hurting me and how she prayed I would forgive her somehow. I did forgive her, but the damage had been done. Sure, we could repair our relationship and find a way to move forward. But what about all the people who had incorrect perceptions about me? How was I supposed to convince them that none of it was true? How was I supposed to fix this whole mess? I was devastated and confused.

Over time, I realized I had to let all of that go. The Bible is pretty clear on what to do: *forgive.* We don't always want to forgive. We want to storm out of rooms, rage against anyone who will listen, hold grudges, and retaliate. But that only hurts us.

In Matthew 18:21–22, the apostle Peter asked, "'Lord, how many times shall I forgive my brother or sister who sins against me? Up to seven times?' Jesus answered, 'I tell you, not seven times, but seventy-seven times'" (NIV).

God knows that we're going to need a lot of forgiveness—both giving it and receiving it. Being in relationship with others means we're going to get hurt and maybe even betrayed at times. But we have to keep forgiving, again and again.

HOW TO PUT LOVE FIRST

Forgiveness is hard, but living with the pain of unforgiveness is harder. Is there someone you need to forgive today? Is there someone you need to apologize to? Prayerfully ask God to help you. You'll find peace in forgiveness.

LIVING FEARLESSLY

For God gave us a spirit not of fear but of power
and love and self-control. 2 TIMOTHY 1:7

SADIE

I WRITE ABOUT FEAR. I PREACH ABOUT FEAR. I TALK ABOUT
fear. I even have a "fearless" tattoo. I do fear-inducing things like
jumping out of airplanes, speaking in front of thousands of people, and
showcasing my amateur dance moves on national TV—not because I
have mastered fear, but because way too often fear still threatens to
master me. If I don't stay clear on who's in charge, fear will overstep
its boundary every time.

Earlier I mentioned I had a very wise woman on my podcast who
said that in her forty-year marriage, the only thing she regrets is the
eight years that she brought fear into her relationship. Fear keeps us
from having healthy relationships. You cannot love freely or fully when
you are afraid of what might happen in the future or if you're afraid of
being rejected or losing someone.

Not long ago, I noticed that one of my favorite people was having
a negative effect on our friend group. I tried talking to him about it. I
tried reminding him of our values and showing him how he was going
astray. Still, he wouldn't budge.

Around that time, Christian and I rewatched the movie *Titanic*.
During the final scenes, as the lifeboats stuffed with people were
leaving, others were swimming in the freezing water. The people on
the lifeboats began to question if they should go back and try to save
others, even if it put themselves at risk. A thought occurred to me: if
our friend group were a part of the *Titanic* incident, would I go back

and save more people with the chance that I might drown, or would I save myself?

I realize this analogy may make me sound like a horrible person for even questioning it. Everyone wishes they would be the person who would go back. But I think it's important to consider: Would fear take over, or would faith?

I eventually sought out my friend. I told him I cared way too much about him to let him destroy his relationships with those of us who knew him and loved him and wanted to be in his life. I told him that regardless of how he chose to act going forward, I was going to love him and pray for him. I continue to invite him into our lives, even though I know he may cause a little drama, but I'd rather risk that than let him drown alone.

Even though I was afraid of this confrontation—of how he might respond, of whether I would be making things worse—God gave me the ability to conquer my fear and fight for the relationship. We might not always be able to banish fear altogether, but we can let it compel us toward love and healing and reconciliation.

HOW TO PUT **LOVE** FIRST

Is fear or faith ruling your relationships? Take a moment to really think about your words and actions toward those closest to you and spend some time journaling about what you think you might be doing out of faith and what you might be doing out of fear.

BEING CONSISTENT

Therefore, my beloved brothers, be steadfast, immovable, always abounding in the work of the Lord, knowing that in the Lord your labor is not in vain. 1 CORINTHIANS 15:58

CHRISTIAN

AS I WAS GROWING UP PLAYING BASEBALL, COACHES always said that "players play like they practice." If we gave 50 percent effort in practice, then we'd never give 100 percent in an actual game. I didn't always love this reality when it was scorching hot outside and we were entering the back half of a long, drawn-out practice, but one thing it did teach me was the importance of consistency. The more consistent we were in practice, the better we played our games.

It's the same in relationships. Consistency matters. Who you are in the day-to-day interactions, in the privacy of home, or in the small things reveals who you will be in the bigger, grander, more long-term seasons. This, in turn, is the key to building a long-lasting, healthy marriage.

One way that Sadie and I can tell whether our marriage is strong or not is by looking at how consistently we're acting on our agreed-upon values—how faithfully we're sticking to them. We try to uphold all the commands in the Bible about how to treat a spouse or another person. So, we assess how consistent we are in considering each other's needs, speaking kindly to each other, resolving conflict quickly and thoroughly, being candid about our shortcomings, making room for each other by being patient and understanding, praying together, and tending to each other day by day. When these things are happening consistently, Sadie and I both feel a sense of safety in our marriage, as though no matter what else is happening in our lives, our connection is sure and strong. But when one or more of these things is off, the whole relationship feels shaky at best.

Case in point: A few weeks ago, Sadie was having a really rough week. She'd been transparent with me about the struggles she was going through at work, and while I cared deeply about what she was dealing with, I must have been distracted for a few days and neglected to ask how she was doing.

The following morning she said, "Babe, would you mind asking me how my heart is and just checking in a little more frequently this week? I need to get better at initiating how I'm really doing, but until then, can you prompt me a little?" She needed me to be more consistent and more present. Of course I said yes and was diligent that week in following up.

The reason that exchange worked is because of our high value on consistency. We want to know each other well. We want to be known well *by* each other too. We're not gunning for total predictability here because how boring would that be? We're shooting for consistency, for practicing the things we've agreed are important to us until they become second nature in our home.

HOW TO PUT **LOVE** FIRST

How well are you upholding the value of consistency in the relationships that matter most to you? Do your family members and intimate friends know they can count on you? Do *you* believe you can be counted on? It matters that people can count on us, not just once in a blue moon but consistently, regularly over time.

DAY 44

TAKING INITIATIVE

Having gifts that differ according to the grace given to us, let
us use them: if prophecy, in proportion to our faith; if service,
in our serving; the one who teaches, in his teaching; the one
who exhorts, in his exhortation; the one who contributes,
in generosity; the one who leads, with zeal; the one who
does acts of mercy, with cheerfulness. ROMANS 12:6–8

SADIE

BEFORE I MOVED BACK TO MONROE, I LIVED IN NASHVILLE
for a while. Although I only knew maybe two people in the whole city
when I moved there, by the time I left, I had a whole circle of life-
giving friends. I loved those girls! Someone was always texting the rest
of us to see if we wanted to get together for a movie night or a girls'
night or a party, which meant that our group was always bouncing
around from one person's house to another's, playing games, hanging
out, having fun.

Then I moved back home.

As soon as I arrived, I was eager to find "my group." I wanted
friends to play games with and study the Bible with and talk about life
with, but it didn't just magically happen. Nobody reached out to initiate anything with me. So I started extending invitations: *Does anyone
want to come over and play games? Does anyone want to go to the movies
with me? How about starting a Bible study with me?* I got some responses,
but it was always on me.

I felt a little frustrated at first over the fact that if I didn't make a
plan, no plan would get made. Maybe it's because I grew up in a home
with a mom who loves to host gatherings and who encouraged me to
make people feel welcome in our home. I'm also the kind of person

who likes having people over. That's when I realized my frustrations with others' lack of initiative were pointing to things I was good at and could do easily.

So, I planned. I arranged. I asked. I hosted. And a whole lot of fun was had by all.

Today's passage from Romans is a great reminder that you and I are called to use the gifts we've been given by God. Think of it this way: if you've been given a gift for teaching but never teach, how useful is that gift? If you have the gift of leadership but never lead, or the gift of generosity but never give, or the gift of service but never serve, what good are those gifts? God would do better to hand them to someone else. There are all kinds of spiritual gift inventories that can help you learn what your gifts are, but here's an easy one-question test: *What is it that you keep wishing someone else would do?*

I'm learning that often the answer to that question is the gifting you possess. I'm gifted at initiating and hosting, so if I'm wishing someone else would do that work, maybe I'm the one who needs to act. Sometimes our frustrations are signals telling us that we're the ones who need to step up.

HOW TO PUT LOVE FIRST

What is it you're waiting for right now? If you're waiting for someone else to organize a get-together, you should organize a get-together. If you're waiting for someone else to raise her hand to serve, be the one to serve. Whatever it is, do it today and let your initiation bless others.

BEING AWARE

While they were talking and discussing together, Jesus himself drew near and went with them. But their eyes were kept from recognizing him. LUKE 24:15-16

CHRISTIAN

I'VE ALWAYS PRIDED MYSELF ON MY SENSE OF AWARENESS. I pay attention to my surroundings. I notice people before they notice me. And I'm quick to replenish things like trash bags or toilet paper or rinse out Honey's bottles.

But we all miss things sometimes. Once, Sadie and I were on a beach vacation with some of our extended family. On our last morning there, I decided to take a spin on a remote-controlled surfboard-type thing called a foil board. Everybody was on the dock watching me take my turn, and as I paddled back on my stomach, I suddenly changed my mind and started riding it away from shore again.

Immediately everyone hollered at me. I was flying on top of the ocean when I heard their yells, and the only thing that made sense to me was that they had spotted a shark nearby. What I didn't know was that over my left shoulder in my blind spot was a giant catamaran quickly coming toward me. We missed each other. Barely.

When I made it back to shore and realized what had happened, I jumped off the board and lit in to my family. I was so mad. Why had they screamed their heads off instead of helping me understand the situation? Underneath my rage was fear. I blew up at my family that day because I'd been shaken to my core. I had nearly died, with Sadie watching from the dock. In my anger, I was completely unaware of how my actions and words were making my family members feel.

So later I went to find Sadie and everyone else to apologize. *I'm sorry. I screwed up. I was scared.* They were trying to alert me, but we had missed each other. Sometimes our lack of understanding of the full picture can become a relational barrier. It can cause us to miss the very thing we're supposed to see—in my case, that my family loved me and was afraid I'd get hurt, or worse.

Just after Jesus' resurrection from the dead, He appeared to two disciples who didn't know who He was. The two were walking along a road outside of Jerusalem (ironically, talking about *Him*), and Jesus showed up at their side. Luke 24:16 says that "their eyes were kept from recognizing" Jesus.

When they made it to their destination and Jesus shared a meal with them, they finally realized it was Him. Jesus. The Messiah. The One God had raised from the dead. He'd been at their side all along, and they hadn't seen it. He'd been present with them the entire time, and they had almost missed Him.

Jesus is with you every moment of every day, whether you see Him there or not. And He is at work in your life, whether you know it or not.

As you think about your closest relationships and how you treat the people in your life, ask God to make you more spiritually aware. Have you been missing something—their unspoken needs, their desire to connect, their deep concerns for you—that you can be more present for and aware of?

HOW TO PUT LOVE FIRST

Write a list of the people in your innermost circle. Pray for awareness of their needs and circumstances, and reach out to one of them today in a tangible way that lets them know you really see them.

LOVING WITH AUTHENTICITY

Let love be genuine. ROMANS 12:9

SADIE

I ONCE HAD A ROOMMATE WHO WAS GOOD AND KIND AND—
much to my initial discomfort—very interested in what was going on
in my life. I'd get home from work, and immediately she'd say, "Hey!
How was your day? What's new at work?"

I'd reply with the usual, "Good! Good. Yeah . . . busy, you know
. . ."

And then I'd ask her about her day with very detailed questions
for her to answer so that the conversation wouldn't come back to me.

I thought this strategy was working well—her asking questions,
me deflecting and hedging and avoiding—until one day after hearing
my usual response, she said, "You always say that, but what does that
mean? I actually want to know what made your day good and what
keeps you busy."

That was a life-changing moment for me.

If you're like me, a lot of people ask how your day is going or how
you're doing, but not everyone truly cares to know. My roommate took
a moment to show me that she actually cared and wanted to know
real things going on in my life, which made me realize the power
of authenticity and what it looks like to have a friend who genuinely
cheers you on.

Remember that super-close friend of mine who betrayed me and
turned my whole friend group against me? Well, one of the by-products
of that ordeal was that I became skeptical of all future friends. I was
scared to draw near to anyone for fear of being betrayed. I became
pretty closed off, and I put a wall up so others couldn't easily get in.

I was everyone's friend from a distance, but I didn't have many close friends at heart level.

I won't lie: It took me a while to heal from that friend betrayal, but eventually I got to where I needed to be. With the help of good friends like my roommate who made the effort to show she really cared, I got to a place where I knew in my heart that it was far better to walk through life risking love than to never put yourself out there at all.

If you're the friend trying to help another person open up their heart, start with intentionality and authenticity. Genuine love goes a long way (Romans 12:9). The more you do that, the more others will begin to trust you.

> If you're the friend trying to help another person open up their heart, start with intentionality and authenticity.

And if you're the one who's scared of getting hurt and has built up walls, try to let people in no matter how scary it may feel. Community is one of God's greatest gifts, and it starts with us being real with each other, even in the mess and the fear.

HOW TO PUT LOVE FIRST

Are you holding someone at arm's length today? Sometimes that's for good reason. Not everyone should be in our inner circle. But sometimes we keep our distance and close ourselves off in unhealthy ways. Is your heart open and healthy? Or too open, perhaps? What step can you take today to move in a healthy direction?

RELYING JOYFULLY ON ONE ANOTHER

If the whole body were an eye, where would be the
sense of hearing? If the whole body were an ear, where
would be the sense of smell? 1 CORINTHIANS 12:17

SADIE

WHEN CHRISTIAN AND I DID THAT LIFE-PLANNING RETREAT
we talked about earlier, part of the interview process involved figuring
out how my husband and I are wired. We were stunned by how totally
different we are. They say that opposites attract, but this felt over-the-
top. He's deeply introverted; I'm extroverted 100 percent. He's a doer;
I'm a dreamer. He's a one-task-at-a-time kind of person; I'm like, "Give
me everything all at once!" He's a planner; I'm super-spontaneous. On
and on it went.

I came away from that weeklong session with renewed clarity for
why Christian sees things so differently than I do, for why he responds
to situations so differently, and for why he always gets irritable when I
load our calendar with too many social things.

I also came away truly grateful because this is exactly as it
should be.

The broader context for 1 Corinthians 12:17 talks about the body
of Christ. When someone becomes a believer, he or she becomes part
of this unified whole. Paul explained it this way: "For just as the body
is one and has many members . . . so it is with Christ. . . . If the foot
should say, 'Because I am not a hand, I do not belong to the body,' that
would not make it any less a part of the body. And if the ear should say,
'Because I am not an eye, I do not belong to the body,' that would not
make it any less a part of the body. . . . But as it is, God arranged the

members in the body, each one of them, as he chose. If all were a single member, where would the body be?" (vv. 12, 15–16, 18–19).

I think Paul was saying the kingdom of God is incredibly diverse, and we each bring something special to the mix. I wouldn't want Christian, or any of my friends, to be just like me. And it's fruitless to compare ourselves to others or condemn them for not being more like us. We have to fight the urge to promote ourselves above others or demote ourselves below them, just because we spot differences between us. The far better way, according to the Bible, is to realize that we're *all* needed.

I have friends who are super detail-oriented and friends who think in broad brushstrokes. I have relatives who have the entire year planned out every New Year's Day and relatives who take life as it comes. I know high-profile influencers who can't get enough of crowds and those whose dream vacation is staying at home.

I'm sure you know people on these spectrums, too, and isn't that a beautiful thing? Just think how boring and predictable life would be if everyone were the same. We need one another—with all our different perspectives and assumptions and capabilities and skills—to accomplish the work God has for us to do. The saying really is true: we may go faster alone, but together, we'll go far.

HOW TO PUT LOVE FIRST

Let someone help you today—step aside to let their gift shine. Or take a moment to point out someone's gift. Tell them what an amazing job they're doing and how grateful you are for them.

IDENTIFYING OUR BLIND SPOTS

He [God] trained us first, passed us like silver through refining
fires, brought us into hardscrabble country, pushed us to our very
limit, road-tested us inside and out, took us to hell and back; finally
he brought us to this well-watered place. PSALM 66:10–12 MSG

CHRISTIAN

HAVE YOU EVER BEEN CRUISING ALONG, JUST LIVING YOUR
life, when suddenly you are made aware of a blind spot you never knew
was there? Just like every vehicle has a blind spot or two, the same goes
for our relationships: blind spots can develop that keep us from seeing
what we need to see. And if you'd like a built-in system for discovering
and dealing with your blind spots, just get married. Spouses can spot
them right away.

I've been thinking recently about my blind spots, areas where my
perspective seems limited, where I'm not seeing clearly all that there
is to see. Here's one of them: *intensity*. I can be a very intense person, and if I'm not careful, that intensity can turn into outright anger,
which usually affects my relationships and always leaves me feeling
regret. One time we were playing Spikeball with some friends, and the
net was super loose and flimsy, so when we'd slam the ball, it would
just die on the net. I was getting annoyed because I should have been
winning these points, and in that moment I sarcastically asked, "Did
a fourth-grader put this together?" Our friend who had assembled it
got embarrassed and flustered, which made Sadie aggravated with
me. Needless to say, we ended up tightening the net, still lost, and it
sparked a conversation about my frustration over the little things.

I'd like to be the kind of person who only experiences what the
Bible calls "righteous indignation," the type of anger that Jesus once

had when He entered a house of worship and saw people selling items in the temple (Matthew 21:12). He wanted it to be easy to find God in that place, but newcomers had to wade through a full-on trade show to get to the sanctuary. He was *incensed*. That's righteous anger. Holy anger. Anger that glorifies God.

The truth is, I get old-school angry. And I'd like for that to stop.

Today's verse reminds us that what the psalmist was talking about happens by divine refinement, by God expanding our vision and perspective until every blind spot is removed. John 15 says He prunes every branch that isn't bearing fruit, so that someday fruit can grow. He heats things up like a refiner's fire until the impurities we hold can be melted away from our lives. And He keeps at it, heating and melting and heating and melting, until all He sees when He looks at us is His reflection, clear as day.

This refining process often happens through the people closest to us, through our close relationships.

Of course, nobody likes to be fixed, pruned, or refined. It's uncomfortable. It's sometimes painful. It's exhausting to truly change. But if we want to experience that "well-watered place" the psalmist was talking about, we'll actually beg God to do that work. And we'll be open to listening to those who love us and want the best for us too.

HOW TO PUT LOVE FIRST

Sit down with someone you trust who knows you well. Ask them to help you identify your blind spots. Ask them to share—with love and gentleness—some things they see in your life that you might be missing.

DAY 49

BEING ACCOUNTABLE

Iron sharpens iron, and one man sharpens another. PROVERBS 27:17

SADIE

IN HIGH SCHOOL I WAS KNOWN AS A "GOOD GIRL"— specifically a good *Christian* girl—and I started believing the lie that it wasn't okay for me to struggle.

Over the years, I've met many people who faced the same dynamic as a teen. Perhaps you were affirmed for making wise choices or for being a person of conviction or for really thinking things through, but later this meant you had nowhere to turn when you acted impulsively, caved to peer pressure, or did something dumb.

I was so scared of doing something stupid that the whole world would find out about. Sometimes the only motivation for me to do the right thing was simply that it was expected of me and I didn't want to upset people by not doing it. It wasn't necessarily that I *wanted* to do the right thing.

As I grew up, I realized that setup did have some positive effects. Yeah, maybe my motivations weren't perfectly pure for why I avoided certain situations, but it did mean I avoided *a lot of unfortunate situations*. The fact that people were watching me may have saved me from untold sorrow and pain.

These days, however, I avoid unfortunate situations because I have accountability in my life. I have a close friend of mine whom I can trust completely. I tell her *everything*. I tell her the awkward stuff, the wins and losses, the fears, the annoyances, and the pain. I tell her some of the thoughts I'm thinking that make me sound crazy. I tell her the things I'm feeling. I tell her my dreams and my devastations and my goals and my plans. And she tells me these things too.

Our conversations aren't always easy, mostly because admitting failure is hard, acknowledging sin is hard, and owning up to jealousy is hard. But our conversations are always helpful in that they remind me who I want to be.

It might seem safer to never risk this type of intimacy—after all, if nobody gets close to you, then nobody can hurt you, right? I understand that, but I still believe that any friendship worth having is worth fighting for.

If you've ever caught yourself eyeing someone else's friendship and wondering how relational intimacy comes so easily for them, just know that it *isn't* easy. If they have an awesome friendship, it's because they work like crazy to make it that way. They practice staying in touch. They practice asking deep questions. They practice giving honest answers. They practice resolving conflict. They practice showing up for each other. They keep coming back for each other again and again because their connection matters that much.

You can have this too. If you don't yet have this kind of ride-or-die friend, the kind of person who will cheer you on whenever you're killing it and call you out and keep you accountable whenever you aren't, ask God to bring this person into your life. Or maybe they are in your life already, and you just need to be vulnerable enough to share. Ask Him to show you who she is. And while you wait on that friendship to surface, work on becoming the kind of person that friend will need and adore.

HOW TO PUT LOVE FIRST

Think about the friends you have in your life right now. Are you truly accountable to any one of them? If not, think about who you might trust enough to develop that kind of friendship.

SPEAKING LOVE

Gracious words are like a honeycomb, sweetness to
the soul and health to the body. PROVERBS 16:24

SADIE

INTERESTINGLY, CHRISTIAN AND I DIDN'T REALIZE THAT
Honey's name was unusual until people started reacting to it. We'd
meet someone while holding our daughter, and when they found out
her name, their expression would shift from delight to confusion.
"Honey? Seriously?"

"Yep," we'd say, our heads nodding. Honey.

It's true that Christian and I were so struck by the words of Proverbs
16:24 that we named our child Honey. The verse says, "Gracious words
are like a honeycomb, sweetness to the soul and health to the body."

But our affection for the word *honey* goes back even further
than that.

Soon after I first met Christian, I referred to him affectionately as
"the boy with the honey words." I even had a honey pot emoji beside
his name in my phone. Our entire dating relationship happened long
distance, and so one of the things we did during our phone calls every
night was to read through the book of Proverbs. There are thirty-one
chapters in Proverbs, which makes it the perfect monthlong read. And
on day sixteen, we got to that proverb about gracious words being like
honeycomb. I paused as I was reading and said, "You speak words like
honey, Christian. They have been sweet and healing to me."

My relationships before Christian had caused me to question my
worth and shut down entire parts of my personality that I could
tell weren't desirable. But with Christian, none of that was necessary.
Through his words, spoken across hundreds of miles, he had brought

me back to life . . . to the life I'd always longed to live. To the fullest version of myself. Isn't it amazing that our words hold such power? When God created life, He *spoke* it into existence. He said, "Let there be light," and there was light. In His case, words literally caused life.

But they can also cause pain and sadness. They have that power too.

People told Christian and me before we got married that marriage can sometimes feel like a massive mirror in front of you. I did not understand what that meant—until I got married. And then, in this other person, I could see the reflection of all of my actions, tones, affections, and words spoken. When I spoke words of affirmation, I could see Christian's reaction bounce off those words with confidence, joy, and love. And then when I spoke with a critical tone or an attitude, I watched as my words tore him down. His body language would change as I stole the joy out of that moment.

Consider how you carry the words that you say. You could encourage someone to be the fullest version of themselves today, or you could really bring someone down. Think about the impact of your words when you speak them. Are they like honey?

HOW TO PUT LOVE FIRST

Have you ever witnessed someone in a fit of anger pause to answer the phone and suddenly turn their voice to sunshine and rainbows? Have you ever been that person? It's funny to think about, but the reality is that our words and tones are not always honey. Let's make a concerted effort today to speak words that show people love.

CELEBRATING THOSE YOU LOVE

Rejoice with those who rejoice. ROMANS 12:15

SADIE

HAVE YOU EVER BEEN SAD ON YOUR BIRTHDAY? IT IS PARticularly hard when there is so much anticipation for this one day, and then the day comes and it's disappointing.

My thirteenth birthday was the first birthday my parents weren't there for. They had a business trip, so I stayed the night with a friend. It wasn't the end of the world, since I was with my friend. However, when it came time for dinner, I was fully expecting to get to pick my favorite place to eat or choose the meal since it was my birthday. But nope, they ordered takeout. I have to admit, I was pretty sad because I really wanted to be celebrated. Yet there I was on my birthday, entering my teenage years, eating takeout with another family.

A couple of years ago, I chose the word *celebrate* as my word of the year to focus on. Typically, my chosen words are a little more convicting or inspiring, and celebrating might seem like just a fun thing to do or be a part of. But I learned throughout that year that celebrating is actually more of a discipline than just a party.

> It's much harder to celebrate and be grateful when life isn't playing out the way you thought it would.

To celebrate something requires you to stop in a moment and give praise where praise is due. It asks you to rejoice with those who rejoice—and that's not always easy. It is easy to celebrate when everything is going your way, but it's much harder to celebrate and be grateful when life isn't playing out the way you thought it would, when things aren't so perfect. And I've certainly had greater disappointments than that thirteenth birthday.

During that year of choosing to celebrate, I had to learn to look past my feelings, look past my disappointments and struggles, and look up. I had to shift my perspective to Jesus because that would take my eyes off me and put them on Him, where I could always find something to celebrate. Sometimes that meant walking outside to look up at the stars, telling God how I felt, and praising Him through it.

Philippians 4:4 says, "Celebrate God all day, every day. I mean, revel in him!" (MSG). What a great call to action—every day, revel in God!

Since that memorable takeout-dinner birthday, my family has made it a point to make birthdays fun, and we find the time to stop and celebrate. My parents are the best party planners in the family, and through their efforts, we have danced, laughed, and sung together. And no matter how we are feeling, we come together as family and friends to support one another and lift each other up. Memories are made, hearts are softened, and life is sweeter.

HOW TO PUT LOVE FIRST

I know it might be difficult to celebrate others, especially when you don't feel like it, but I encourage you to practice the spiritual discipline of celebration and rejoice with those who rejoice. Who can you celebrate? What can you celebrate? If you can do it today, do it! If it requires planning, do that instead.

BEING FAITHFUL

Therefore we must pay much closer attention to what we have heard, lest we drift away from it. HEBREWS 2:1

CHRISTIAN

SADIE AND I WERE IN AN AIRPORT RESTAURANT RECENTLY, waiting to board our flight, when we overheard a man talking to his buddy in very descriptive language about a certain female country singer's body. We immediately felt uncomfortable, and as we walked away to find another spot to wait, Sadie said, "I can't believe that guy. He had a wedding ring on!"

I could tell she hadn't recognized the guy, but I had. He's a famous professional athlete and is married to an equally famous actress.

We were both bothered by the conversation, not only because it was crude to the singer, but it was also dishonoring to his wife, who wasn't there. For him to sit there and fantasize about another woman—especially in such a shameless and public way—was demeaning. I don't know a lot about this person's marriage, but from the few comments I heard, I questioned its foundation.

Sadie and I believe marriage is a reflection of Christ and the church, and we're trying to build a strong foundation now in these early years to stand on for the rest of our lives. And the best way to have a strong foundation is to be intentional about how we invest our time, energy, attention, affection, and conversation. We want to prioritize our time together now so that we don't wake up one day and realize that we've unintentionally drifted apart.

So we work on projects for LO together. We go out on dates together. We pray together. We parent Honey together. We play tennis together. There's a *lot* of togetherness. This keeps us connected and committed, and it helps our foundation remain strong.

The writer of Hebrews said that we should "pay much closer attention to what we have heard, lest we drift away from it" (2:1). Left to my own sinful nature, I never "drift" in a Godward direction. I don't drift toward a perfect, connected marriage. I don't drift toward goodness or selflessness or humility. I don't drift toward patience or love. It's only by God's grace in my life that *any* of these things show up. And this is true for you too.

We're all prone to drifting, to forgetting what we've learned.

So, how do we keep from drifting from our foundation? Let me give you a few practical ideas.

If you are at the gym, and a woman comes into your area wearing something that catches your attention, you probably need to relocate to wherever she is not.

If you're accessing porn on your phone on bathroom breaks, you need to leave your phone outside while you go to the bathroom.

If you're connecting emotionally—in person, through texts, online—with someone who is not your girlfriend or spouse, you need to exit that relationship. Consider going to a counselor instead.

You get the idea. We have to be intentional about not letting ourselves drift from the life-giving presence of God. We need to be the kind of person who is faithful—to our God, to our spouse, to ourself.

HOW TO PUT **LOVE** FIRST

Do you need some safeguards in your life to help you be faithful, to help you keep your eyes on God? Odds are you can already identify what areas in your life cause you to stumble the most. What safeguards can you put into practice today that can steer you in a healthier direction?

ASKING FOR GOD'S HELP

"Ask, and it will be given to you; seek, and you will find;
knock, and it will be opened to you. For everyone who
asks receives, and the one who seeks finds, and to the
one who knocks it will be opened." MATTHEW 7:7-8

CHRISTIAN

ONE NIGHT SADIE AND I WERE WATCHING ONE OF OUR
favorite cheesy shows on Netflix, the kind of show you watch only to
laugh at. Generally, when we do this, I can count on an hour of funny
back-and-forth between Sadie and me, but this
time she was silent. I'd crack a joke and side-eye
my wife: nothing. Finally, I paused the show, put
down the remote, turned toward her, and asked,
"You okay, babe?"

> If I had to nail
> down the most
> frequent prayer
> I've prayed,
> especially
> regarding my
> relationships,
> it's this one:
> "God, help me."

With all of Sadie's responsibilities—
conferences, preaching, the podcast, her team at
LO, her roles as wife and mom and daughter and
friend—I knew she'd been stressed. So for the next
fifteen minutes I listened as she vulnerably and
honestly put words to all that stress. While I listened, I asked God for help.

Throughout my walk with Jesus, if I had to nail down the most
frequent prayer I've prayed, especially regarding my relationships, it's
this one: "God, help me."

God, help me be quick to listen and slow to speak.
God, help me do and say the right thing.
God, help me choose patience . . . gentleness . . . grace.
God, help me show Your love.

Sitting beside Sadie that night, her feeling overwhelmed and on the brink of tears, I asked God to help me know how to help my wife. And He told me to help her the same way that He's always helping me: *Help her bear her burdens. Help her carry this load.*

So I said to Sadie, "I don't have a super-busy schedule this week. How can I help? Tell me what I can take on. I'll do whatever you ask me to do."

The look of relief that came over her was undeniable.

I could have ignored my wife's obvious stress and just kept the show rolling, hoping she would get past whatever was bothering her and join me in laughing at the TV. But I would have missed a huge opportunity to be Jesus in her life, in the same way that she's been Jesus to me a thousand times. In a matter of twenty minutes, we'd shared a burden together, come up with some solutions, and hit a new depth of connection as a couple. I was able to help when she most needed it.

This is exactly what God does for us. He comes to our aid at just the right time. He shares our burdens and sees what we need. More patience? Extra compassion? A way forward? He's right there ready to help when we ask.

If we ask for His help, He'll offer it. He'll give us insight. Wisdom. Perspective. Creative ideas. We simply need to ask.

HOW TO PUT LOVE FIRST

What person close to you could really use your help right now? Is there someone you need to spend twenty minutes listening to, encouraging, and offering to carry some of their burdens? Ask God to help you know what they need.

SPEAKING LIFE

Though your sins are like scarlet, they shall be as
white as snow; though they are red like crimson,
they shall become like wool. ISAIAH 1:18

SADIE

AFTER I EMERGED FROM THE ANGSTY THREE-YEAR
relationship I talked about before, I remember being shocked by how
long it had taken me to finally break free. Sometimes we don't know
the gravity of a situation until it's in our rearview mirror—this was
definitely one of those times.

For many months I grieved the person I'd become over those three
years: skittish, indecisive, insecure, afraid. Who was I now? How could
I return to myself—or at least the version of me I wanted to be?

Around that time, I went on a ski trip with some friends. We were
staying at a cozy cabin, and one morning I saw the most stunning view
of the fresh snow, and I was leveled by a Bible verse that sprang to
mind. It was a message delivered from the prophet Isaiah to the people
of Israel, who'd made a habit of disobeying God. (I could relate.) Isaiah
said this: "Come now, let us reason together, says the LORD: though
your sins are like scarlet, they shall be as white as snow" (Isaiah 1:18).

I stood there stunned. Teary.

Did God really see me—in spite of all that disobedience, all that
disbelief, all that waywardness, all that clinging to a relationship—as
snow-white? If He did, it was only because of Jesus. And that day,
because of Jesus, I believed that this was true for me. That God really
does see me as white as snow.

Fast-forward two years, after I had met Christian and started falling in love; we had invited him to come on our annual family ski trip. I

had told him the story of looking out at the snow that day and the Lord speaking that to me, and he said, "Well, I can't wait to get there and remind you of what He said." Sure enough, he and I were heading to the top of the mountain on the gondola when he turned to me, took in the glistening ground below us, and said, "That is how God sees you, Sadie." I got to speak those words of life right back over him as well. We were two sinners sitting on a chair lift amazed that God saw us as pure as snow because of Jesus and repentant hearts.

There were so many things Christian could have said to me right then, throwaway things that would have meant little to me. The fact that he chose to speak truth to me then is something I will never forget.

When we say something true to another person, those words have a divine effect. They speak life. They pour in courage. They remind us of what's real. They foster God-honoring intimacy. They draw us in. It is one thing to believe something for yourself, but it is so powerful when someone believes something with you. When you take time to listen to people's dreams and desires and come alongside them to believe with them, powerful things happen.

HOW TO PUT LOVE FIRST

In previous generations, when people were in love and were sharing private moments, they'd share what were called "sweet nothings" with each other, those little whispered sentiments that only they would hear. Today, when you have a moment alone with your person, I hope you'll deliver not a sweet nothing but a *sweet something*. Speak truth to them. Speak meaning. Speak life.

HANGING OUT ON PURPOSE

Look carefully then how you walk, not as unwise but as wise,
making the best use of the time, because the
days are evil. EPHESIANS 5:15–16

SADIE

IT HAS BEEN SAID THAT WE ARE THE SUM OF THE FIVE people closest to us. That means that the more we hang out with people, the more *like them* we will become. We'll start to talk like them. We'll start to dress like them. We'll start to think like they think. We'll be shaped by their influence in our lives. And the same is true for them: they will also be influenced by us.

When I moved back to Louisiana after having been gone for a few years, I remember feeling like a totally different person. So much about that environment was familiar to me—my family, the church I grew up in, the streets and shops and sights—but I had completely changed. I wasn't a middle-schooler trying to find her way in the world; I was married, a soon-to-be mom, and the leader of a ministry I loved. In one sense, I "knew" tons of people—I had childhood friends who were still in town and had dozens of extended family members who made Monroe feel like home. But the reality was that on the friendship front, I was starting all over again.

Not knowing what else to do, I decided to start a Bible study and invite any girls who I knew, with an open invitation for them to invite friends as well. Now as I look back, it is crazy how many of my closest friendships came out of that Bible study. In my life today, I see rich relationships on every side. That was such a longing of my heart, and I know it is the longing of so many of your hearts—and it can be hard to find. I want to encourage you that God answered my prayers by giving me women who love me and deeply love Him—but He answered that through my obedience to open up my own doors and invite people in. It is easy to get stuck in this idea of waiting to get invited somewhere or waiting on a friendship to magically appear, but a lot of times it starts with our inviting and creating a place where friendship can grow.

I bring this up because I want to give you permission to evaluate your closest friendships and see how many of them are helping *you* grow. If you and your besties don't consistently come away from interactions with one another feeling mutually uplifted, encouraged, emboldened—maybe a little challenged, even—then it might be time to dig a little deeper when it comes to friendships and relationships. After all, you are becoming more and more like the people you are with!

> I want to give you permission to evaluate your closest friendships and see how many of them are helping *you* grow.

HOW TO PUT LOVE FIRST

Take a sec today to think about the five people who are closest to you. What are you learning as you hang out with them? Who is that causing you to become?

STICKING TOGETHER

Two are better than one, because they have a good reward
for their toil. For if they fall, one will lift up his fellow.
But woe to him who is alone and when he falls and has
not another to lift him up! ECCLESIASTES 4:9-10

CHRISTIAN

STRESS CAN DO WEIRD THINGS TO PEOPLE, AND WHAT I'M
about to share proved that in some really challenging ways.

Honey was sick—really sick. Our young daughter was in trouble,
we weren't sure what was wrong, and we were standing in an empty
hospital corridor completely clueless about what to do. Sadie was
almost paralyzed by fear, and I was spiraling down into anger's awful
grip; she and I weren't in good places.

Sadie was calling everyone we know, eagerly asking them to pray. I
was pacing and fuming, intent on the sole goal of getting my kid out of
that hospital bed. Life as we knew it had totally
stopped. What were we supposed to do now?

> When I encounter stressful situations, I turn to anger. It's a cover for fear, and a poor one at that.

I look back on that night and wish I'd done
things differently. It wasn't that I did anything
wrong; it's just that I also didn't do much right.
When I encounter stressful situations, I turn to
anger. It's a cover for fear, and a poor one at that. I
get mad—at the situation, at myself for not being
able to turn things around, at life. When Sadie
encounters stress, she turns to anxiety. You could
say that both of us get afraid, and you'd be right.
But because we're both operating in our chambers of fear, we neglect to
see the other one's predicament and help usher in some peace.

I've always been interested in the whole foxhole-friends concept. It's the idea that when you go through something really traumatic with someone, such as when two soldiers dodge enemy fire in a trench for days on end, you emerge as intimate friends. You've faced down an oppressor and lived to tell about it, and now you'll forever have each other's backs. And while I think that dynamic is true in marriage as well, sometimes it takes a minute to get there, to that "more intimate" state of mind.

Back to what I wish I'd done differently. Yesterday, Sadie and I were replaying that terrible time when Honey was so sick, and we didn't know how to help. I thought about that hospital stay, about my anger, and about Sadie's fear. I asked her, "What do you wish I'd said or done that I didn't say or do?"

She didn't even have to think about it. "I wish you'd wrapped your arms around me and reminded me that no matter what happened, we were going to be okay."

Comfort. Reassurance. Words of encouragement. That's what she'd needed from me that night when I'd had nothing at all to give.

When life pulls the rug out from underneath your feet, it's tough to have enough self-awareness to respond like you hope you'd respond. But here's what I'm learning: when we're willing to circle back after the dust has settled and ask what would have made things better, that's when we get to learn the things that we wish we'd known all along. That's when two people start living as one.

HOW TO PUT LOVE FIRST

Today, ask a loved one about a past stressful exchange, about what you might have said or done to make things better instead of worse. What can you learn from their insight about how to respond when the next stressor hits?

GUARDING YOUR HEART

"The good person out of the good treasure of his heart produces good, and the evil person out of his evil treasure produces evil, for out of the abundance of the heart his mouth speaks." LUKE 6:45

SADIE

HAVE YOU EVER WONDERED WHY YOU KEEP CUSSING EVEN when you don't really want to be the cussing type? Or why you keep being rude to that one person, even though you don't see yourself as rude? Have you ever wondered why you keep getting defensive or aggressive or domineering or inappropriate when you're around that one specific friend or group?

This verse in Luke 6 has always been convicting to me because it basically says, "Hey, if you can't figure out why you keep saying the wrong things, then *hellllooo*, check your heart."

In other words, the reason stuff sometimes comes out wrong is because we're putting the wrong stuff in.

> If you want to show up in all the relationships in your life as a generally positive and life-giving person, then you can't drown yourself all day long in negativity and dark stuff.

If you want to show up in all the relationships in your life as a generally positive and life-giving person, then you can't drown yourself all day long in negativity and dark stuff. Let me get real for a sec. If the songs you always listen to are vulgar and the TV shows you always binge are crude, then what comes out of you in your real-life conversations will be equally vulgar and crude. Either that, or you're going to have to spend a ton of energy censoring yourself as you try to present yourself as someone you're not.

There's a much easier way: stop welcoming the negative in.

I'm serious. I know it seems impossible to steer clear of all the junk that's out there today, but it absolutely can be done. I can't tell you how many shows I've started with total enthusiasm, only to abandon them three episodes in. Why? Because I started noticing that my thoughts were changing. And my words were changing. And my anxiety level was changing. My heart was changing. And *not* in a positive way.

Here's the opposite scene, played out: when I'm careful about what I put into my heart, I'm pleased with the words that I speak. When my mind and my heart are steeped in truth, truth is what comes out of my mouth.

I'm not going to sit here and tell you that this is some earth-shattering idea because it's not. "Garbage in, garbage out" has been around forever. But here's the thing: if we aren't careful to do the hard work of stepping away from not-excellent things, we will eventually become not-excellent ourselves, and nobody wants that. This is a simple lesson to learn but a hard lesson to live out.

HOW TO PUT LOVE FIRST

Take a look today at what you're letting into your heart—music, media, beliefs. How is all that stuff shaping the words that you speak? How is it shaping the person you've become?

CALLING YOURSELF OUT

So whoever knows the right thing to do and fails
to do it, for him it is sin. JAMES 4:17

SADIE

HAVE YOU EVER GOTTEN SUCKED INTO WATCHING A SERIES
that in your heart you knew wasn't doing anything good for you? One
episode leads to the next, and before you know it, you're hooked. It's
not *so* bad, you tell yourself. Or that's what I did, anyway.

For me, it was a reality show about people falling in love, and
yeah, while the f-word was thrown around pretty casually, and the
relationships didn't exactly follow any kind of biblical narrative, it was
really entertaining to watch. *This is giving me great insight into how the
world views dating,* I'd tell myself. *I'm gaining good insights here . . .*

Smooth, right?

Around that same time, I was watching a Brooke Ligertwood
sermon online and was so struck by her words that I paused the video,
rewound it a few seconds, and watched again. She said, "Compromise
is convincing yourself that it is okay to do the wrong thing if it is for
the right reason."

Wait. Was she calling me out?

I cannot even tell you the last time I felt so much *conviction.* It was
as if she was talking straight to me. I'd been compromising more often
than I cared to admit—not just in watching a show that was question-
able at best but for other things as well. And while other forms of godly
input hadn't stopped me in my tracks, this one had. I'd been busted,
and I knew it. I needed to let go of that series and move on.

One time I read about how people who are trained to identify
counterfeit money study only the genuine thing. They study real

bills so intently that whenever they come across a counterfeit bill, they know it right away. The little lie I'd been believing was that by studying the world, I could learn more about Jesus. Crazy, right? We don't learn about Jesus from studying the world—we learn more about Jesus from study the Word.

> We don't learn about Jesus from studying the world—we learn more about Jesus from study the Word.

It is so important to pay attention to the Holy Spirit's activity in our lives. Know what triggers you. Know what tempts you. Know what tries to pull you away from the person you long to be. Is it physical intimacy with someone you're dating? Is it alcohol? Is it coarse language or off-color joking? Is it a show that pushes the boundaries a little too far? Go ahead and call yourself out, so someone else doesn't have to do it for you. Because odds are no one else will do it for you. It is the Spirit's job within you to convict; it's your job to respond to Him. Whenever you sense that God is nudging you to move away from darkness and toward His light, turn and head that way.

HOW TO PUT LOVE FIRST

Conviction is a good thing—a great thing! But when I'm ignoring something God is telling me to do, or not do, or I'm trying to rationalize something, it can leave me feeling tense, short tempered, and defensive—not exactly shining qualities and definitely not traits that will help me grow in my relationship with God or others. If you're feeling convicted about something, stop and pray. Call a trusted Christian mentor and ask for their help and prayer too.

BEING REAL

Lying lips are an abomination to the Lord, but those
who act faithfully are his delight. PROVERBS 12:22

SADIE

IN JOHN 12:1-8, THERE IS A STORY TOLD ABOUT A WOMAN
named Mary who poured a full pound of expensive oil onto the feet of
Jesus and then wiped his feet with her long hair. This was a wild thing
to do, the equivalent of dumping a gallon of really nice perfume onto
the floor. The room would have smelled amazing, but what a waste,
right?

Well, that's exactly what one of the disciples named Judas thought
that day. He was there in the room as Mary did this crazy thing and
said, "Why was this ointment not sold for three hundred denarii and
given to the poor?" (v. 5).

Despite his noble-sounding question, Judas didn't *actually* care
about the poor. The real reason he said what he said, according to
verse 6, was that he "was a thief, and having charge
of the moneybag he used to help himself to what
was put into it."

Judas was hiding his selfish ways with
spiritual-sounding smooth talk. But Jesus wasn't
here for it. He basically said, "Leave her alone. You
could learn a thing or two from this woman about
how to worship me with authenticity and generosity and grace."

I know there's a lot of talk these days about
who is an "influencer" and who is not, but the truth
is that we're all influencing *someone*. We have to

> I know there's
> a lot of talk
> these days
> about who is
> an "influencer"
> and who is not,
> but the truth
> is that we're
> all influencing
> *someone*.

make sure that influence is pure. So, what is it for you today? Are you leading people from a place of conviction and service? Or are you faking it until you (hope to) make it someday?

Let the fruit of your life tell the story of someone who was honest in her pursuit of God, who was honest about her shortcomings (and successes!), who was honest at every step along the way. Honestly, the world needs more honesty. Proverbs 20:7 says, "The godly walk with integrity." And what freedom it can bring in a filtered world to walk in pure integrity.

HOW TO PUT **LOVE** FIRST

If you've been faking spiritual success lately, stop. Find one person to tell the truth to today. Trust God to show you the path forward. Begin now getting real—with God, with your friends, with yourself.

KNOWING LOVE GROWS

Keep your heart with all vigilance, for from it flow
the springs of life. PROVERBS 4:23 ESV

SADIE

I KNOW FIRSTHAND WHAT IT'S LIKE TO HAVE MY HEART
broken. To have my trust broken and to feel betrayed and shattered
to my core. That is exceptionally hard to recover from. Especially if
these things happen from no fault of your own.
And when they do, it's so difficult to love and trust
again. If that's been your experience, I want you
to know that I see you, and I understand. I'd also
like to take your hand and help you walk forward
to place where you can know that love grows, it
multiplies, and it can spill forth in abundance.

> Love grows, it
> multiplies, and
> it can spill forth
> in abundance.

When Christian and I had Honey, it was the most amazing,
breathtaking experience. It was, and then some, every good thing
everyone had ever told me about being a parent. A deep, incredible
love for this child burst forth from me. Parenting is the hardest, most
stretching, most challenging thing—and yet sometimes I can hardly
fathom this great love I have for my child.

While writing this devotional, I found out I was pregnant with
our second baby. And again, my heart burst. And the amazing thing is,
I didn't have to make room in my heart for this new child. The spaces
in my heart did not divide; that's the miracle of love—it multiplies.

I know you may be thinking, *sure Sadie, but those are your babies.
That's different.* And I get that. But I think the principle can apply to all
our relationships. I think our hearts can be places where love multiplies
for all kinds of people in our lives.

Does this mean we hand over our hearts to everyone? No. Our verse for today says, "Keep your heart with all vigilance." The New International Version says, "Above all else, guard your heart." *Above all else.* We must guard our hearts.

First Thessalonians 3:12–13 tells us, "May the Lord make your love increase and overflow for each other and for everyone else, just as ours does for you. May he strengthen your hearts so that you will be blameless and holy in the presence of our God and Father when our Lord Jesus comes with all his holy ones."

May God strengthen our hearts. May he strengthen each one of us and make our love increase and overflow for each other and everyone else. Friend, I hope this is your experience. That you allow God to hold your heart and let it overflow with love.

HOW TO PUT LOVE FIRST

What are some fears you have that are holding you back from letting love multiply? Write them down and give them to God today.

PAUSE AND REFLECT WITH
DR. JOSH KIRBY

WELL DONE. YOU'VE MADE IT ANOTHER THIRTY DAYS ALONG in our journey. Over the past month, I imagine you have had some changes in your closest relationships. In the relationships that we hold nearest to us, there is never a moment in which we are standing completely still. They are ever evolving. My hope is this devotional is welcoming a shift—a new and clearer focus—in these connections. A relationship only needs one person to initiate change. So, take heart in knowing God can use *you* to make a positive impact in others, and He is using this time to draw you nearer to Him.

MATURING IN LOVE

One of the reasons relationships are continuously shifting and changing is because we humans can be pretty complex beings, and we are all different. Put two people together with different expectations, family backgrounds, coping mechanisms, Enneagram numbers, and favorite Netflix shows to binge, and you get a complex relationship. Suffice it to say, all relationships involve complexity. There is no magic formula for life that fits everyone. What is important in our relationships is that we honor differences and recognize when we are too caught up in having all the right answers. This allows us to see that, despite our differences, we are all created for love, in God's image.

Unfortunately, many of the ideas about love that come from outside in our culture or from within our own self-interests are focused on feelings and are far from God's original design. Love, of course, can and does evoke feelings—and very important feelings in the right context. But love is not a feeling. It is something that is chosen, lived out, and built in promise to one another and with one another. God's love is already built perfectly, and intimately from beginning to end. Ours is not. What Paul is telling us about love in 1 Corinthians 13:4–5 is that this is what God is like and what Jesus, whom Paul encountered, is like. It is our standard; yet we, in God's love, must faithfully return to love, again and again.

As we grow in God, we grow, in love, because God *is* love. If we are made in His relational image, then maturation in following Christ will *always* produce better relationships. In a close relationship, you will go through challenging situations together. For long-held relationships, you will literally face the worst of life together. It is in these times that we mature. This is God's promise to us. We hold fast to Him, not just because today may be tough but because we know some "tomorrow" in the future will be. In a spiritually healthy relationship, we work to build confidence in a shared promise to hold to each other when obstacles arise. As we mature in Christ and with others, we are better able to delay our impulses, take responsibility for them when we do act upon them, and look ahead without fear because we have a promise.

> As we grow in God, we grow, in love, because God *is* love.

OUR PROMISE AND GOD'S FAITHFULNESS

In a marriage, a couple makes vows to one another. These are promises to hold fast to, often written out, and read in front of relatives and friends. Many couples will take part in premarital counseling or a marriage class to discuss and prepare for potential roadblocks along the way. However, I don't know many couples who write out detailed plans for what they will do when those vows are really needed. The reason they don't is that that is the point of the vow. In *The Meaning of Marriage*, Tim Keller explains: "Wedding vows are not a declaration of present love but a mutually binding promise of future love." The vow is the plan.

There is a point in every close relationship, though, where it feels the only thing holding it together is a vow, promise, or understanding that we will work through whatever it is in front of us. We will all experience some measure of doubt, anger, fear, or *stuckness* with our most trusted and needed people. It is in facing these tensions, whether brief moments or long seasons, that God shows us His faithfulness and gives us the presence to love one another, as He loves us. This is where we are at our best. Not because we are strong, but because He is.

DEEPENING AND STRENGTHENING
OUR RELATIONSHIPS

Building closeness and intimacy is about being seen, known, and accepted for who we are, in our most vulnerable states. This is God's nature in being with us and how we long to be in our closest relationships. Most of us will only share that experience with a small number of people across our entire lives. We strengthen our bonds with others in small increments, steadily, over time, not unlike the lifelong process of maturity in our spiritual journeys. As we do this, it inherently draws us into greater security in our relationships, as in our faith. We don't have to force it. God allows it to emerge within us as we focus on putting Him and love first. We must, however, be intentional in our focus. The incremental moments that create deeper and stronger relationships involve our ability to communicate openly and reconcile genuinely.

Communicating in love involves sharing our hearts and receiving others in theirs, fully accepting them in the relationship. This does not mean we do not confront someone when we are concerned or hurt by them. Nor does it mean we approve of everything they do or remain in a relationship if ending it is a necessary boundary. It does mean that we see them as worthy of grace, and whether we remain loyal to them or learn to let them go, we believe that God can work in and through them.

Remind yourself regularly that the important people in your life were created in God's image. Ask God to help you respond to them from this perspective the next time you see them. It will make a difference. Seeing others through God's creation reminds us of the reverence we should have for Him, the fear of God that the Bible speaks about. This fear, in love, moves us toward Him and others, not away. We are more able to stay present, listen, and be curious with our friends, family, and spouses rather than respond out of our own concerns and motivations.

> Remind yourself regularly that the important people in your life were created in God's image.

In a relationship where two people work to consistently communicate with grace and honor each other's God-given gifts and personality, there will be more positive and peaceful moments. But no relationship is spared from times of disconnection. We often talk about the highlights, the Instagramable parts of life, but you cannot pose, smile, and filter your way to closeness. It is how we repair tension and conflict that strengthens our relationships. Most of us can identify when our pride surfaces. Sometimes we will resist it and fail to recognize what it's like to be on the receiving end of us. That can be vulnerable, for sure, but taking responsibility for our behavior and influence on a relationship is critical. If we want a dynamic to improve, ultimately, it only will when we participate in the reconciliation.

One of the insights that comes to light for many people in counseling is that they are actually fearful of the presence of conflict itself. This fear can lead them to avoid or resist reconciliation, even though they ultimately desire it. Often, they come into adulthood without having had a model for healthy conflict management in their families of origin or past relationships. The presence of conflict and tension, however, is not the problem. In counseling, I use the metaphor of someone learning martial arts. To become skilled, you must learn to embrace falling on the mat because you will find yourself there at times. For those who have not seen healthy examples of this, it can be daunting to learn that conflict is not something to fear. But as we do, we grow to realize that talking through those moments, even if we are still hurting or feeling tension, is a sign that the relationship is working as God intended.

People who have weathered the storms of life together for years, growing in intimacy, are masters at attuning to even the smallest of ruptures. It's not because they enjoy them; it's because they fully embrace opportunities for reconnection and living a life with others as God loves us in our imperfections. God gave us the ministry of reconciliation in sharing the gospel with the world, to disciple others toward Him and eternal safety in His saving grace. I believe this translates all the way down into the smallest moments of repair in our relationships as we live out God's call with others.

RHYTHMS FOR LOVE

We are all creatures of habit and operate within patterns. So do our relationships. Our personal patterns of thoughts, feelings, and behaviors influence a shared relational cycle that develops as we do more and more life with one another. When we are relationally more safe and secure, we feel more balanced. We can move toward each other to connect and grow closer while also respectfully holding boundaries to maintain our autonomy. But maturing close relationships require healthy, purposeful rhythms to remain balanced from season to season. Rhythms serve as reminders that ground us and bring us back to what is most important: love.

Love is something we must practice regularly. When we do, love endures. There will be seasons in a relationship that require more effort, like when we are going through a difficult period of stress, change, or loss. As we navigate the hills and valleys of life, it is important that we create rhythms for rest and renewal to remain engaged with others. Spending time to be still and calm is vital for the overall health of our minds, bodies, and souls. For some, regularly talking things out with a professional or pastoral counselor can be helpful.

For others, it may be spending purposeful time alone. Taking care of ourselves is taking care of our relationships.

As we navigate life with our closest people, in happiness and heartache, we are also creating ongoing testimonies of God's faithfulness. In growing with others, we can always find a redemptive and resilient story. Again, this is God's promise to us in putting love first. Perhaps you've written or shared your personal spiritual testimony. Ask your spouse or your closest friend if you can write your relationship testimony together. Return to it from time to time when you need inspiration or reconnection. Our testimonies remind us that, through God's guidance, we can overcome and do great things with others by our side.

> Love is something we must practice regularly. When we do, love endures.

If you look at the stories of the people in your life who are the most content, fulfilled, and resilient in their relationships, you will often find they are not just people who manage life's challenges well. They are also consistently taking time to nurture their hearts through ongoing emotional and spiritual encouragement. These relational rhythms become healthy boundaries that help protect the relationship from outside stress and care for one another to build trust within. See if you can find time over the next week with someone you are seeking to grow closer to and discuss how you can establish a new rhythm together. It can be simple, like scheduling a regular meetup at a coffee shop to offer support and prayer for one another. Anything new takes getting used to, but once you start to see the fruits of these moments, you will begin to look forward to them as balancing forces in your relationship.

When we are putting love first, we are more able to see and know that God intended our relationships for meaning and purpose. And while we play a part in them, He is in control, and He is our ultimate security. He is always there, waiting for us to return to His faithful promises as we live out our stories in our most meaningful relationships.

As you move into the final part of the book, Sadie and Christian will help you see how when we are rooted in love with God and our closest relationships, we are able to have influence in our greater community, in our communities of faith, and with those yet to come to know Jesus.

PART 3

YOUR RELATIONSHIP WITH YOUR COMMUNITY

BEING IN ALIGNMENT WITH GOD

So God created man in his own image, in the image of God he created him; male and female he created them. GENESIS 1:27

CHRISTIAN

I ALREADY KNOW THAT IF A NEW MARVEL MOVIE IS COMING out, Sadie and I have plans that night. We do not miss Marvel premieres.

When I was asked recently what the best Marvel movie is, I had to pull up a list of all the contenders on my phone and really give that question some thought. It all depends on how you want to define "best." Are we talking "best" in terms of groundbreaking plot? Or "best" in terms of cinematography, which I'm an absolute nerd about? Or "best" in the sense that if you could only see one Marvel movie in your lifetime, you should totally see *this one*?

I suggested *Infinity War*. The characters are authentic with their motivations and flaws, the emotional journey is at its most intense, the cinematography pushes the envelope, and the movie ends on a perfect cliffhanger. Marvel made a perfect film with that one.

I say all this for a reason: when you love the creator, you love what the creator creates. Since I love Marvel, I have been committed to seeing just about every film they put out.

In the same way that I value those movies because I've come to value the brand that puts them out, if you and I value God, then we will value all that He creates. We'll value the natural world—animals, plants, trees, and everything that inhabits the earth. More importantly, we'll value people—the crown of all He's made.

There are two implications here. First, if we believe that we were created by God—on purpose and for a purpose—then instead of fixating on who we think we are and who we think we want to be, we'll prioritize His perspective on things. We'll ask, "What did You have in mind when You created me, God? Who do *You* want me to be?"

A lot of confusion would be resolved today if everyone would risk asking those two questions and then aligning with what God says is true.

Second, if we believe that others were created by God, then that divine imprint is the first thing we should notice about them.

I'm as likely as the next guy to get frustrated with people as I go about my day. I like things to run smoothly. I have a plan that I don't like to deviate from. Other people have a way of messing up my plans, and it can be hard to see that divine imprint in those moments.

But this verse from Genesis is such a important reminder to me. When I get annoyed or short tempered with someone, I'm getting short-tempered with someone made in the image of God. Because I love the Creator, I need to love all of His creation, even the annoying and hard-to-love ones. When I stay in touch with how deeply I love God as Creator, I find I deeply love His creation too. And this, it seems, is a wonderful first step to building community.

HOW TO PUT **LOVE** FIRST

Marvel movie challenge day! Find someone who needs a pick-me-up, grab some takeout or snacks, and enjoy a Marvel movie together. One of our favorites is *Captain America*! Pair that with some popcorn and M&M's, and it's bound to be a success.

BE COMPELLED

Then Jesus told his disciples, "If anyone would come after me, let him deny himself and take up his cross and follow me." MATTHEW 16:24

SADIE

OCCASIONALLY I'M ASKED TO COME SPEAK TO GIRLS WHO are in juvenile detention centers, and it's an experience I always love. The girls are open to encouragement, open to truth, and open to a little impromptu dancing, which is my favorite thing to do.

Not long ago I was teaching a group of girls at a detention center when one girl in particular caught my eye. She began to really lean in and ask me questions—tough questions that expressed why she had a hard time believing there is a God. I appreciated her questions and her honesty, and it led me to sit with her week after week and answer questions and pray with her.

We had great conversations, and I could tell she was serious about wanting to follow Jesus. By the end of the seven-week series that I was leading, I had the privilege of baptizing her. Afterward, I got a prompting from God. *Give her your Bible*, He said, which totally caught me off guard.

I don't know how you feel about your Bible—I don't know if you even have a Bible—but for me, my Bible is like a security blanket. I take it everywhere. I write in it constantly. I know how it got every single smudge, stain, and rip. I'd been given my Bible at my high school graduation, and as part of the gift, every member of my family had written their favorite verse and a note to me inside the front cover. This Bible was like a close friend.

Still, God was clear: *Give your Bible to her.* And so I did.

I'll be honest: I cried the entire drive home. But just *after* I finished crying, I had an amazing thought: That girl was young in her faith and had never read a Bible before, and now she basically had a road map for how to navigate God's Word. I'd highlighted key verses. I'd made margin notes explaining what things meant. There were tons of cross-references noted where I'd written down other places in Scripture where similar themes were explored. That Bible meant so much to me; was it possible it would mean even more to her?

> Sometimes God compels us to move, to act, or to give something up for His kingdom.

Jesus was once approached by a rich young ruler who wanted to know how to inherit eternal life. Jesus told him to go sell all his possessions and give the money to the poor. The rich young ruler "went away sorrowful, for he had great possessions" (Mark 10:22).

I was sorrowful, too, when I was asked to give my Bible away! But sometimes God compels us to move, to act, or to give something up for His kingdom. The satisfaction of following Jesus—whatever that requires, whatever sacrifices must be made—is far greater than the satisfaction of holding on to earthly things. When we deny ourselves instead of indulging ourselves, we're free to follow Him.

HOW TO PUT LOVE FIRST

Is there a book or Bible you could give to someone today? Something that's really impacted you that you know could help someone you care about? Today, let's give a favorite book or Bible to someone—whether it's already well loved or newly purchased.

BE CURIOUS

Let each of you look not only to his own interests, but
also to the interests of others. PHILIPPIANS 2:4

CHRISTIAN

I GREW UP ON THE GULF COAST OF FLORIDA, AND I SPENT
pretty much every spare moment I had near the ocean, on the ocean,
or in the ocean. When you practically live in the water, it's only natural
that you develop a great curiosity.

If you've ever gone snorkeling, then you know that when you're
bobbing in the ocean above the water line, you can see some pretty
amazing things. The water expands around you as far as your eye can
see, rays of sunshine glisten on the ocean like sparkling diamonds,
seagulls dart in and out of the waves in search of their lunch. It's a
cool scene, no doubt. But if you really want to see something spectacu-
lar, you have to dip your head under the surface. It's unbelievable, the
activity going on just below the water's surface: all kinds of fish swimming this way and that, plant life in every color imaginable, clusters
of seaweed, stingrays, and so much more. Above the water line everything is peaceful and quiet, but a single inch under the surface, and it's
a whole different world.

These days everything is so automated and everyone is so busy
that if we're not careful, we'll blow through an entire day without really
interacting with another human being. Have you noticed this? You
give a slight head nod to the guy scanning your card at the gym but say
nothing. You mumble "Thanks, man" to the Starbucks barista or the
DoorDash delivery guy but pay no attention to his name. You post the
latest evidence of your awesomeness but don't take time to comment
on how incredible others are.

From an efficiency standpoint, we're killing it. From a spiritual one, not so much. If we want to impact our world for Jesus, we need real connection, and curiosity is a great place to start. We have to dip beneath the surface, which is where things get really interesting.

When the apostle Paul explained to the believers in Philippi how to be more like Jesus, one of the things he told them was to look not only to their own interests, "but also to the interests of others" (Philippians 2:4). This sounds so simple, but if people were already behaving that way, why would Paul have needed to say it? We need this message every bit as much as they did. We need to be reminded to look up—from our circumstances, from our phones, from our lives—every once in a while and check out what's going on in the lives of the people around us.

"Look to the interests of others." The first step to being like Jesus is to *look*. It's to see people.

And then to be curious about their lives. There are a thousand interesting things to learn about every person you encounter, if only you'll get curious enough to ask.

HOW TO PUT LOVE FIRST

Today, as you encounter colleagues or people in the world, take the time to really talk to them. Ask how their day is going. How their family is doing. What they're looking forward to. What they've been up to lately. You never know where a conversation and some kind curiosity might take you.

DAY 64

BE COMPASSIONATE

Finally, all of you, be like-minded and show sympathy, love, compassion, and humility to and for each other. 1 PETER 3:8 THE VOICE

CHRISTIAN

I WAS DRIVING ON A BUSY ROAD ONE AFTERNOON WHEN A car pulled out in front of me, and I had to slam on my brakes to avoid hitting it. If I had glanced down for even a split second, I would have plowed right into the back of that car at about fifty-five miles per hour. My heart was pounding, and rage kicked into high gear. *What kind of idiot was behind the wheel of that vehicle? How on earth did they ever get a license? Learn to drive!*

As I moved into the left-hand lane to pass the car that had almost made me wreck, I noticed an elderly woman in the driver's seat, her eyes squinting as she looked ahead of her.

Another time, I went through the drive-thru of a local ice cream shop near our house and placed my order. Nothing outrageous, nothing complicated. Just a milkshake mixed with chocolate and chocolate chips. How hard is that?

But after I had left the drive-thru, as I drove down the highway, I discovered that I'd been given the wrong order. *How incompetent can a person be?*

Or how about the time I was scrolling through my Instagram feed and saw a post from someone who was clearly looking for sympathy. *Dude, can't you pull it together at least a little bit before you jump online and post?*

Now, it's possible that that lady shouldn't still be driving, that the fast-food staff should double-check orders, and that some people shouldn't be so quick to post their emotions online. But what I started noticing after enough of these experiences had piled up was that the real issue wasn't with them. The real issue lived in my heart.

A popular story in Scripture is found in Mark 6, where Jesus fed five thousand people. The part of that story that gets my attention has nothing to do with loaves and fishes; it has to do with Jesus' heart. He had just come ashore and noticed a great crowd had gathered to hear what He had to say, and He "had compassion on them, because they were like sheep without a shepherd" (v. 34).

To Jesus, it didn't matter who they were, what they did for a living, or what any of their present challenges were; He had compassion on them.

So when I encounter faceless or nameless people every day, why is it so hard for me to have compassion? I regularly forget that there is a *driver* inside every car that enrages me, that there is a *human being* involved in every errant fast-food order I pick up, that there is a *person* behind every social media post that irritates me.

There is an owner for every incessantly barking dog.

There is a coworker attached to every missed deadline.

Behind every frustration, irritation, and mess, we find a person—a living, breathing soul God cares deeply about. A person Jesus came to redeem. In a lot of cases, a person who might really be struggling with something.

What if we approached every situation from a place of compassion first and then went from there? Compassion before context—I'm working to get there. You too?

HOW TO PUT LOVE FIRST

Today, when you feel any kind of annoyance toward someone, give grace to that person. It might require you to receive God's grace first before you can extend it to someone else.

BE INTENTIONAL

Love one another with brotherly affection. Outdo
one another in showing honor. ROMANS 12:10

SADIE

DO YOU EVER FIND YOURSELF STUCK WHILE TRYING TO
make a decision? Here are a few of my recent debates:

- Should I find a babysitter so I can get some work done, or should I just hang here with Honey this afternoon?
- Should I stay up with Christian and watch a movie, or should I head to bed and get some extra sleep?
- Should I spend some extended time with God by reading His Word, or should I scroll my feeds to see what's going on in the world?

Decisions, decisions, right?

Many of us gained an awareness about how we make decisions during the pandemic. One of the most profound things I took away from that season was that if I didn't intentionally schedule time to get together with other believers and study God's Word, it would get shoved aside for other things.

When the world first shut down, my priorities became watching the news, playing games with my family, and taking naps. But as those weeks turned into months, it became evident to me that if I didn't reevaluate my priorities, I could spend my life stuck in neutral and lose sight of what matters to me.

That was a place I did not want to be, so I invited a few girls to our house to pray and study the Bible. And as we all showed up week after week, our friendships were strengthened and our intimacy with Jesus deepened. It all stemmed from that tiny little step of me saying, "Hey, I need prayer and God's Word in my life. I should gather some girls."

In the examples I listed here, there's no clear right or wrong choice. There's nothing wrong with working for a couple of hours or cuddling Honey all afternoon. There's nothing wrong with watching a movie with my husband or getting some extra sleep. The same goes for reading the Bible and scrolling Instagram: it's obviously better for me to read Scripture, but it's not necessarily bad to hang out online for a few minutes. So, if neither answer is wrong, then how do we know what's *right*?

We can start by determining whether the time we give something truly matches our priorities. If your priorities include close relationships where you invest in each other's spiritual lives and growth, then some of your decisions need to include cultivating those relationships.

Christian works out with a buddy of his every Saturday morning at seven. Our family heads to my parents' house on Sundays. We always have our friends over on Wednesday nights to hang out in fellowship. We FaceTime Christian's parents every day.

Whatever you do—a Friday morning hike, a post-church brunch on Sundays—take time to prioritize the important relationships in your life. If you don't, they'll get shoved aside for whatever is easiest or seems most urgent. I've found that when relationships lose depth and closeness, it's not usually because we don't have time for them. Rather, we let our lives run all over us instead of being intentional about how we'll show up and who we'll show up for.

HOW TO PUT LOVE FIRST

Jot down the names of the five or six people who are most important in your life. Then underneath each name, write out three or four things those people love to do. Once you have your list, schedule some "dates" with them.

BE FRUITFUL

Do your best to present yourself to God as one
approved, a worker who has no need to be ashamed,
rightly handling the word of truth. 2 TIMOTHY 2:15

CHRISTIAN

DO YOU BELIEVE WE NEED A PERSONAL RELATIONSHIP WITH
Jesus to be effective in our other relationships and the community of
people around us?

I would have answered that question much differently five or six
years ago. Before I yielded my life to Jesus, I thought I had solid community. I was in college. I had friends. I had fraternity brothers. We
"did life," and I thought things were going smoothly. We never talked
about spiritual matters, but that didn't bother me at the time.

Fast-forward to a conversation I had recently with a guy I regularly
see at the gym. After we chatted a bit, I asked him where he went to
church. He proceeded to say he hadn't been since Covid. Several weeks
later, he saw me at the gym and asked me to get coffee and talk about
Jesus.

That sequence of events may seem inconsequential, but for me it
represents real progress. During my college days, I didn't care if the
guys I hung around were growing spiritually, serving others, and being
faithful to God.

But now? Those items are at the top of my list.

Nothing gets me more excited than having a spiritual conversation
with someone who wants to make strides in their relationship with
Jesus. And because those conversations matter so much, I find myself
spending a ton of time preparing for them. I read the Bible often so
that I can present myself "to God as one approved, a worker who has

no need to be ashamed, rightly handling the word of truth." I listen to sermons and music to inspire me. I reach out to friends to see how we can pray for one another.

I've always been drawn to John 15:5, where Jesus talked about abiding in Him. He said, "I am the vine; you are the branches. Whoever abides in me and I in him, he it is that bears much fruit, for apart from me you can do nothing."

Without Jesus, I *am* nothing. Without Jesus, I'll *do* nothing. God doesn't ask us to be popular or rich or famous. He asks us to be *fruitful*, to bear fruit in whatever we do—and it's hard to be fruitful in isolation. He wants us to abide in Him and let His love flow in and through us for our good and also for the good of others.

> Nothing gets me more excited than having a spiritual conversation with someone who wants to make strides in their relationship with Jesus.

HOW TO PUT LOVE FIRST

What can you do today to bring life and abundance to your relationships and your community? How can you be open to a conversation about God?

BE EMPOWERED

Little children, you are from God and have overcome them, for he who is in you is greater than he who is in the world. 1 JOHN 4:4

SADIE

CHRISTIAN AND I WERE AT AN EVENT IN NASHVILLE recently, and after it ended we decided to grab some food with a few friends, even though it was almost midnight.

Christian and a friend of ours had gone ahead to the restaurant to put our order in, and I planned to head over a few minutes later. We were told this place had great burgers, but as I reached the parking lot, I decided this plan wasn't such a good idea after all. I had assumed we'd be hitting a local burger joint, but this was a full-on bar—and a sketchy one at that. Christian texted me from inside, saying, "You're not gonna like this place," and as I tentatively climbed out of the car and went inside, I knew he was right. Everyone was drinking. The whole place smelled like smoke, and the music was blaring. The lights were turned way down low. Not my kind of vibe.

As my friend who recommended the place happily made her way toward us through the crowd, I wavered between disappointment and anger. This girl and I had the same values. And *this* is where she chose to hang out at midnight?

After everyone was done eating, I confronted her about it.

"You seemed really comfortable there," I started. "That whole scene . . . it doesn't bother you? You don't feel out of place?"

She shared that not only did it not bother her, but the place had purpose for her. She explained that when she was young, someone came to talk to her class about human trafficking and about how young girls were being trafficked in her hometown. For the rest of the class, she sat at her desk and *sobbed*. She couldn't handle the thought that this was happening in her own zip code and she did not know about it.

She said she felt like God told her she would grow up to be light in the darkness, that through her presence, she'd help rescue some of those girls. "I always have the most amazing God encounters when I go to places like that bar," she said. "I could never stand in front of thousands of people and preach like you do. But this? This, I can do."

As believers in Jesus, wherever we go, we bring His full power to that place.

In 1 John 4:4 we're reminded that as believers in Jesus, wherever we go, we bring His full power to that place. Since age five, I've also believed I'm on a mission for God—in my case, to preach truth to people who don't know Him yet. And while I still get nervous whenever I'm about to go onstage, I never question whether I'm where God wants me to be, doing exactly what He's asked me to do.

Is your calling taking you to hard places? If so, know that God's power will always meet you there.

HOW TO PUT LOVE FIRST

If you haven't served in hard places, where is a place that you feel led to be a light, even if it might be uncomfortable? Maybe it's in your friend group, in a nursing home, with your family, at a shelter, or on a mission trip. Together, let's go where He calls us.

BE GENTLE

"Come to me, all who labor and are heavy laden, and
I will give you rest. Take my yoke upon you, and learn
from me, for I am gentle and lowly in heart, and you
will find rest for your souls." MATTHEW 11:28-29

CHRISTIAN

A FEW WEEKS AGO A BUDDY OF MINE AND I WERE RUNNING
on a track at a public park. We had planned on a pretty tough workout,
and the track is generally a place where you can run fast and hard.

On this particular day, I noticed that up ahead of us, a couple of
guys and a girl were spread out across the entire track, just mindlessly
walking and laughing, paying no attention to anyone but themselves.
As my friend sprinted toward them, one of the guys jumped into his
lane, nearly causing him to lose his stride and wipe out. I watched the
whole thing unfold, and as I passed the guy who was laughing over his
antics, I said, "Hey, stay in your lane," and I kept on running.

Five years ago, had that same situation occurred, two things would
have happened: first, I would have stopped running and delivered my
"stay in your lane" threat right to the guy's face, spit pelting him in the
eyes; and second, I would never have thought twice about doing so.
"The guy had it coming," I'd say.

That's not what happened this time. This time, I knew better.

I knew to keep on running so that things didn't escalate. And
then I knew to have a little talk with myself afterward because maybe
I shouldn't have said anything at all.

Ironically, that morning I was reading in Matthew 11 where Jesus
talked about people coming to Him to find rest. Then He followed it
by saying, "I am gentle and lowly in heart" (v. 29).

At first that might not sound very appealing. Who wants to be known as gentle or lowly in *anything*?

We want to be strong. Independent. Proud.

We want to speak our minds when we feel slighted. We want to tell the guy on the track to back off and stay in his lane.

We think *gentle* equates to weakness, to inadequacy, to a light touch. In fact, when you look up what "gentle" originally meant in this verse, it's more like *ridiculously powerful while still being wisely restrained*. Jesus basically described Himself as being strong and also totally self-controlled. That's what we're called to be as well.

When I was angry on the track that day, I could have been even more wisely restrained, but I thank God that I've come so far from where I used to be. Day by day, He is making me a gentler person, and there is nothing weak about that.

I've been asked before about the legacy I hope to leave someday, and I'm gaining some clarity there. I'd love to be known as a good listener, an understanding person, an all-around fun guy. I'd love to be known as someone who is kind and compassionate. But the more I think about how Jesus described Himself, the more I want to be known as a *gentleman*, in the truest sense of the word—undeniably strong while being totally self-controlled, the ideal intersection of both.

HOW TO PUT **LOVE** FIRST

Think about the legacy that you want to leave. What is it that you want others to remember about your life? Knowing what you want your life to be marked by can help you make wise decisions in those everyday moments.

DAY 69

BE WELCOMING

So reach out and welcome one another to God's glory.
Jesus did it; now you do it! ROMANS 15:7 MSG

SADIE

ONCE, WHEN A FRIEND AND I WERE HUNGRY LATE AT NIGHT, the only thing open was the local fast-food place, so burgers and fries it was. We pulled around to the window to be greeted by a guy who had to be six-foot-five and over three hundred pounds wearing fake eyelashes, brightly painted fingernails, and a smile from ear to ear. He was a *presence*.

With his big smile, he shook his head and mouthed the words, "We ran out of food! We're closed!"

Seeing our disappointed reactions, he opened the window, leaned out, and said, "Girl, we've been waiting on a truck all night, but it never showed. We ran out of everything! I'm so sorry, but we had to close."

Laughing, my friend and I declared, "Oh, no! You can't be closed! We're hungry over here!"

He joined our laughter and said, "I know, I know! It's terrible!"

Since no one was behind us, my friend put her car in park and asked what his name was.

"Jeremiah," he answered.

"Jeremiah?" I said. "Did you know your name is in the Bible? It says that God has plans for you, and that those plans are for your good! He wants to give you a future and hope. Isn't that cool?"

Jeremiah looked at us for a second, and then said, "You girls want some fries?"

For the next twenty-five minutes, the three of us sat there at the drive-thru window eating french fries, drinking soda, and talking

156

like we were old friends. It turns out Jeremiah had been staying away from church because his grandma had died and he'd been mad at God. Church reminded him of her, and it made him too sad to go.

I offered him a different way of thinking: "Jeremiah, what if instead of choosing to be sad when you went to church, you chose to be glad about what God has done? That there is a heaven. He loved us so much that He sent His Son to die on a cross for us, so that we could have a future and a hope—an eternity spent with Him, where there is no more death or pain."

To that, Jeremiah offered us a funnel cake. We gave him a huge tip, and with full stomachs and full hearts we drove away.

Our night didn't go the way we thought it would. Who knew that a late-night drive would introduce us to this man with such a huge heart and smile, who needed a reminder of God's love? It was a God-ordained connection, and I'm so glad we were able to meet, share a laugh, and talk about God.

Do you live your life with eyes open for opportunities to welcome a stranger or connect with someone you've just met? How can we show love in these unpredictable and spontaneous moments?

HOW TO PUT LOVE FIRST

During our time at the window, we prayed for Jeremiah's mama, who was in the hospital with cancer. It was a beautiful experience and a reminder for me to always be prepared to pray for others, even strangers. Today, let's pray for strangers around us, and if God gives us the opportunity to pray *with* them, let's take hold of it.

BE ENTHUSIASTIC

Now who is there to harm you if you are zealous
for what is good? 1 PETER 3:13

SADIE

WHEN I FIRST STARTED MY MINISTRY, I USED TO WRITE THE
number ten on my hand every day. This was a reminder that whatever
room or situation I entered, I had the opportunity to bring the energy
level up to a ten.

My mom has always been my greatest teacher, and when I was
growing up, she used to remind my siblings and me that we controlled
our moods and the energy we brought into a place. She would say,
"Don't dictate the weather." By this she meant that if we were in a bad
mood, we needed to keep it to ourselves. We could talk to a trusted
friend, we could talk with her or my dad, but we were not to walk into
a classroom at school or onto the basketball court during practice and
negatively alter the emotional weather in that place. We could bring
the mood up, but we must never bring it down.

These days when I show up at work, I've almost certainly had a
rough night of sleep. Honey had colic when she was a newborn, and
she's still not a great sleeper. Christian and I trade off middle-of-the-
night duties, but even when he's "on call," my sleep is disjointed at best.
It's just the season of life we're in.

And lack of sleep is a big drain on enthusiasm.

Each day, I have a choice to make: I can drag myself into the
office, complaining about the wretched night I've had, or I can give
myself an extra few swipes of under-eye concealer, take a deep breath,
send up a prayer for God's strength, and choose to be cheerful instead.
I try my best to make that second choice.

I'm not saying that you and I should fake our way through our days and be sunshine when we feel like a storm cloud. Not at all. We need space to process our moods and emotions. And we definitely need a few trusted confidants we can vent to. I'm simply suggesting that once we've said our piece, had our moment, it's time to start living again. It's time to wake up and stand up and show up with enthusiasm for the work God has given us to do.

> It's time to wake up and stand up and show up with enthusiasm for the work God has given us to do.

In 1 Peter 3:13, Peter reminded us that no harm can befall us when we're staying zealous for what is good. I love the word *zealous*. It means fervent, passionate—*obsessive*, even. To me, that word is permission. It's a word that says, "It's okay to love what you do, and it's okay for it to show."

Even when we're tired.

Even when we're hungry.

Even when we're totally overwhelmed.

It's okay to love this life we're living, and it's okay for it to show. Your mood affects those around you! Consider today how your mood and countenance are shaping your interactions.

HOW TO PUT LOVE FIRST

What room can you walk into today and level up the atmosphere? What group of people in your life need a laugh, some encouragement, or cookies? Never underestimate the power of bringing someone some cookies. Let's get creative and brighten our interactions today.

BE OPTIMISTIC

All the days of the afflicted are evil, but the cheerful
of heart has a continual feast. PROVERBS 15:15

SADIE

EVER SINCE I WAS A LITTLE KID, I HAVE BEEN AN OPTIMISTIC
person: if the glass was half empty, I'd see it as half full, and if the glass
was half full, I'd determine to get it to overflow. I was simply living
with a happy heart. I still live that way today.

When the day isn't going my way and is filled with little annoyances, I think about how it is going to turn into a message from God.
*What are You doing, Lord? What do You want us—and me—to learn from
this? What good will You bring from this situation, and how can I play a
part?* This is how I am wired.

Christian has a lot of good qualities, but optimism is not something he claims to have. One of the funniest stories of Christian and I
dating was when we had an argument behind a magazine stand in the
airport. Yep, you read that right. But it didn't just end there.

We got to the airport early that morning for a last-minute trip
and were just going to see if we could get some tickets to Florida to
be with Christian's family. In my mind this plan was foolproof and
was going to go perfectly. But Christian was thinking about the one
million things that could go wrong.

Sure enough, we got to the airport, and they didn't have enough
tickets, so Christian had to get on standby. He could not stop stressing,
and in his stress, he asked about a thousand what-if questions. "What
if there is no room on the flight?" "What if I can't get home tonight,
and y'all have to stay with my parents by yourself?" "What if I get stuck
in the airport for hours?"

I took Christian behind the magazine rack and basically told him he had to chill. I encouraged him to be a little optimistic! I was so sure it would work out. Finally, Christian went up to the ticket booth for the hundredth time with his one thousandth question, and the guy said, "Here. Take this ticket. You are annoying me so badly." I cannot even tell y'all how hard that made me laugh.

Now I know that sometimes optimism can be annoying when it's overdone, but I think it's way better than stressing over every detail of life. Optimism won't always change the outcome, but it can change the mood in a room or another person's day. Proverbs 15:15 says that "the cheerful of heart has a continual feast." We can provide a feast of sorts for others. However, I'll also readily admit that optimism without God's truth attached to it can become toxic. People don't want fake comments about hard realities if they don't have any meaning or hope behind them. But with eternal realities factored into the picture, there is *always* goodness to be found.

Listen, things can always get better. Things often *do* get better! Chances are things will work out. And what a gift to know that God is actively working to turn things for good in your story. So let's take the idea of optimism to a much deeper level and call it hope! Your hope through the hard situations will show others the faithfulness of God in your life.

HOW TO PUT LOVE FIRST

Who in your life needs to hear that things are going to get better? How can you actively make it better for them? What words of hope can you send them that are rooted in truth?

DAY 72

BE LOVING

And he [Jesus] said to him [a lawyer who was trying to
challenge Jesus], "You shall love the Lord your God with all
your heart and with all your soul and with all your mind. This is
the great and first commandment. And a second is like it: You
shall love your neighbor as yourself." MATTHEW 22:37-39

SADIE

SOMETIMES I FEEL LIKE MY SOCIAL MEDIA ACCOUNT IS A
little bubble of goodness. The people I follow are all such wonderful
people, doing such good things, and posting such encouraging
thoughts. I try to do that with my page as well. But when I look around
the world today, sometimes it's hard to see any love.
I see people with very strong opinions, offering up
those opinions in very harsh ways to people who
may or may not want to hear them. I see a level of
division that is heartbreaking. But I also see a lot of
opportunity to love God and others well.

> There is really only one measure of whether I'm succeeding or not: *Am I loving others well?*

Increasingly, I hold the conviction that despite
all the goals I have set and all of the things I am
trying to accomplish, there is really only one measure of whether I'm succeeding or not: *Am I loving
others well?*

Love God, Jesus said. Love others. Let your life be known by one
thing: *love*.

There is no greater aim in my life than to introduce people to Jesus
Christ. God compels me to do so—to show others love in the fullest
form. Christ is my Savior, my Redeemer, my Friend—and He can be

that for everyone. I want others to find the fulfillment that He alone can provide.

Unfortunately, many people don't want to know Jesus because of . . . Christians. Which is really sad and messed up. Instead of compelling others to know and love God, we often preach a more religious gospel than the relational one that Jesus lived out. We can present a message that feels like an attack, that is so off-putting that others run in the opposite direction.

Jesus didn't shame people to Him. He spoke in love and grace, and people were drawn to Him. When people encounter love like Christ's, they are compelled to follow.

Think back on your own spiritual journey: Were you drawn toward God by being shamed or by being loved? We have a real opportunity before us today, which is to love like Jesus loved. For me that means:

I don't want to cause division in my circles of influence.

I don't want to unintentionally stir up strife.

I don't want to repel people from the message of Jesus.

I want to consistently draw them to Jesus with my message.

God compels us to love—Him first, then others—and the two are connected. When we love others, we show God we love Him too. And when we love God with our whole hearts, it draws people close to Jesus. And there is nothing like His love.

HOW TO PUT LOVE FIRST

What could we start doing to love others and attract them to Jesus? What do we need to stop doing that could be stirring up strife or repelling people from Jesus?

BE TEACHABLE

I will instruct you and teach you in the way you should go; I will counsel you with my eye upon you. Be not like a horse or a mule, without understanding, which must be curbed with bit and bridle, or it will not stay near you. PSALM 32:8-9

CHRISTIAN

OCCASIONALLY, I ANSWER LISTENER QUESTIONS ON MY *4:8 Men* podcast. One guy asked me how I led my family. I think he was looking for a formula or even book recommendations. But what I said was this: "I try to be teachable—that's it."

Being teachable isn't just important within a family context; it's a good quality to have in all areas of community life. If I'm a leader who lacks humility, I'm a bad leader. If I'm a husband who lacks compassion, I'm a bad husband. If I'm a father who lacks tenderness, I'm a bad father. None of us are naturally talented or gifted in every area or in every role; we have to *learn* how to grow and lead. If I'm not willing to be a learner, then I will be bad at every role I fill. But the flip side is also true: when I quit trying to defend my "expertise" and instead show up with a teachable spirit, I can thrive as a husband, father, leader, mentor, son, and friend.

I'm not going to lie: it's tough to maintain a teachable spirit. Our culture prizes certainty. But I bet if you were to name the people you love being around most in the world, the ones who breathe life into you most consistently, they're probably the most teachable, curious, self-effacing, generous, unpretentious people you know. We *love* being around those people. And their teachable spirit is contagious.

Here's what I'm learning about becoming more teachable in my own life: as I practice this privately with God, asking Him to instruct me and show me the way I should go, I'm more willing to learn from the people I'm around. Submission begets submission. As I lay down my vast knowledge (ha!) during my times with the Lord and pick up His wisdom instead, I am more willing to hear what others are saying, to hear the wisdom someone else can offer.

Today's verse uses the image of a stubborn mule who insists on going its own way. We are often that mule, and God is saying, "Listen, I have wisdom to impart to you, if only you'll submit yourself to My ways." He longs to instruct us. He longs to teach us. He longs to show us which way to go. But first we have to admit that maybe we're not so smart after all. Imagine what our churches and communities would be like with teachable, servant leaders. Our homes. Our schools. Social media!

When I'm willing to learn and to be taught, and have my own understanding challenged, it helps my relationships and community. Instead of holding on to my stubborn will and my understanding of what's the best or right thing, when I allow myself to be teachable, I'm actually far less miserable than if I insisted on knowing it all.

You can always be right and always be miserable, or you can be teachable and live at peace.

HOW TO PUT LOVE FIRST

One way to stay teachable (and humble!) is to try our hands at something completely new to us. Invite a friend to try something new with you—a new sport, a new small group at church, a new workout program, a new hobby—something to grow your connection and teachable spirit.

BE PREPARED

"Don't be in such a hurry to go into business for yourself. Before you know it the Son of Man will arrive with all the splendor of his Father, accompanied by an army of angels. You'll get everything you have coming to you, a personal gift." MATTHEW 16:27–28 MSG

SADIE

EVERY DAY OF CHRISTIAN'S AND MY ENGAGEMENT, I thought nonstop about our wedding day. My thoughts drifted to wedding prep—my dress, the pictures, my hair, the whole wearing-a-ring-with-elbow-length-gloves situation. The day was going to be *epic*, and I didn't want to get there and realize I'd neglected an important detail. I wanted everything to be perfect.

I was even waking up at 5:50 *in the morning* so that I could start my workout by 6:30. Please know this: I *love* my sleep. Before having Honey, I did *not* do mornings. But to prepare for my big day, I was up and at 'em, busting my butt in the gym long before the sun started to rise.

I got my eyebrows professionally shaped. I got my upper lip waxed. I got my *arms* waxed, for heaven's sake. Hair and nails were a whole thing, and I was extra careful about what I was eating so that I didn't show up on my wedding day with dull, broken-out skin.

And I don't regret a moment of it because that's what a bride does for her groom. I was preparing myself for Christian and this day that would mark the rest of our lives.

I've always loved studying how different cultures handle wedding preparations. In the Jewish culture, the groom would go away during the "betrothal" or engagement period to make ready a home for his new bride, as we talked about back on day 20. She had to get herself ready. She would bathe. She would put hydrating oil on her skin and hair. She would wear her nicest clothes. She would put on her finest perfume. And she wouldn't just do this upon hearing that her groom had been spotted outside the city and was returning soon. She'd do it *every single morning*, just in case he chose that day to come back.

I think this is a beautiful picture of how we're supposed to live the Christian life. Today's verse reminds us that Jesus is coming soon. He's coming back to get us after preparing a place for us in our eternal home (John 14:1–3), and the last thing we want is to be caught unprepared when we see His face at last.

How do we spiritually prepare for this big day? We've got to live life eagerly anticipating that *today* might be the day when Jesus returns. So what exactly does that mean for our relationships and our community? We can connect with God every day so that we can be reminded of how much He loves us and how His power can flow through our lives, and even into the lives of others. We can connect with the people in our lives, treating them with humility and kindness, forgiving them quickly when things get sideways between us. We can help others get ready by guiding them to a relationship with God. We can stay consistent in our spiritual practices so that the watching world sees light in our lives.

All of life is preparation, friend.

Be sure you're prepared today.

HOW TO PUT LOVE FIRST

Our greatest preparation for this life and the next is knowing and loving Jesus. Whether in prayer or reading God's Word, let's spend extra time with Him today.

BE INFLUENTIAL

"You are the light of the world. A city set on a hill cannot be hidden. Nor do people light a lamp and put it under a basket, but on a stand, and it gives light to all in the house. In the same way, let your light shine before others, so that they may see your good works and give glory to your Father who is in heaven." MATTHEW 5:14-16

SADIE

EVERY MORNING WHEN I PUT ON MY MAKEUP, HONEY watches me. She sits on the counter right beside me, she looks into the mirror to see her chubby legs and silly smile, and she pretends to put on makeup too. She holds a brush in her fist, swipes her cheeks with imaginary blush, and then looks at me as if to say, "Right?"

It's the cutest thing ever.

It's also a little frightening.

Honey only learned to do that by watching me. I am a huge influence in her life, and I've learned I need to steward that influence carefully.

Sometimes I picture her as a teenager texting on her phone while I'm calling her name—because she's seen me on my phone her whole childhood and she's copied my behavior. That vision keeps me off my phone a little bit more whenever I'm around her. The last thing I want her to think as she grows up is that her mama was too busy on her phone to pay attention to her.

It's critical that we're mindful of our influence on those younger than us, our kids, and each other. How carefully do you manage the influence you have in your friends' lives or in the lives of your family and community? Whether you intend to or not, you *are* influencing them.

In the Sermon on the Mount, Jesus reminded His followers—which includes us here and now—that we are the light of the world. We're not supposed to slink around in the shadows; we're supposed to shine brightly for all to see. We have the ability to greatly influence our world for good. This means using our words to build people up, not tear them down. It means using whatever resources God gives us to solve the problems that He wants solved. It means using our energy to bring Him glory instead of trying to earn praise for ourselves. If you're a believer, you can influence someone to love Jesus more fully and to follow Him more closely.

Likewise, we're all *being influenced* by somebody, and we need to make sure that influence is guiding us in the direction we want to go. I talk to people all the time who think they have to be famous to be an influencer, but that couldn't be further from the truth. I can almost guarantee you that the people who influence you the most are not the ones with the "likes." The people with the greatest impact on your life are your friends, your family, your neighbors. Your people at school or work. The couples who come to your movie nights. The people you see every week at church. The people who pick up the phone and call you.

Take a close look at *those* guys and girls. They are the ones who are leading you closer to God and spiritual maturity—or in the opposite direction—influencing who you're becoming day by day.

HOW TO PUT LOVE FIRST

Let's look at who we're following on social media and take a moment to unfollow those who are fostering negative thought patterns, actions, or habits. From now on, be mindful about whose influence you're allowing in your life.

BE HONEST

Rather, speaking the truth in love, we are to grow up in every
way into him who is the head, into Christ. EPHESIANS 4:15

SADIE

CHRISTIAN AND I ARE IN A STAGE OF LIFE WHERE IT FEELS
like all of our friends are getting engaged. If you're our age, you
probably can relate. If you're older than us, you likely remember those
days. Nearly every week, someone we know is popping the question
and sharing their amazing engagement videos on Instagram—and it's
awesome. We love seeing so many people in love.

But with a few of those newly engaged couples, we've seen some
red flags start to fly. This is when things get tricky. Our friends are so
excited to be planning their wedding and want to talk about nothing
but those wedding plans. Are we supposed to come in like a Debbie
Downer and spoil their once-in-a-lifetime fun? Is this the time to
deliver some hard truths, even if it will help them in the long run? It's
agonizing when we want to say something but don't know how.

Because of what we're seeing with our friends, Christian and I
have been having a lot of conversations about honesty. Is honesty really
the best policy? If so, is it *always* the best policy? Is it ever too late to
be honest? Is it ever inappropriate to be honest? When is the best time
to be honest? What is the best approach to take?

So many questions! The conversations have gone deep.

When Jesus walked the earth, He taught His disciples that freedom was found in truth. Not just any made-up truth, mind you, but
His truth, the truth of His Word. In John 8:31–32, He said, "If you
abide in my word, you are truly my disciples, and you will know the
truth, and the truth will set you free." Jesus really did mean that when

we are truthful—when we're honest—freedom will be found. No matter how hard or painful it is to shoot straight, freedom is on the other side.

In my opinion, it's far better to tell someone the truth when they're engaged than watch them learn it after they've said "I do" and the stakes are exponentially higher.

It's far better to hear the hard truth from a friend rather than have that friend ghost you in frustration because you're unknowingly doing something wrong or hurtful.

> When Jesus walked the earth, He taught His disciples that freedom was found in truth.

It's far better to hear the truth from a spouse before resentment starts to take root and robs your home of peace.

I would rather have my heart broken over what's real and honest than continue to live with a lie.

I've seen God do *amazing* things when people were willing to risk being honest with those they care about most. If you're craving greater freedom in your relationships, telling the truth is a great place to start.

HOW TO PUT LOVE FIRST

It is no easy thing to speak hard truths in love, but we think it's essential to godly relationships. Do you tend to be brutally honest without the love, silent without the truth, or perhaps blatantly dishonest? Ask God to free you to speak both truth and love in a way that honors Him.

BE HEALTHY

Or do you not know that your body is a temple of the Holy Spirit within you, whom you have from God? You are not your own, for you were bought with a price. So glorify God in your body. 1 CORINTHIANS 6:19–20

CHRISTIAN

BY NOW YOU KNOW THAT I'M A HEALTH AND FITNESS fanatic, that nutrition and exercise are huge parts of my life. But as much as I love thinking about, talking about, and practicing healthy habits, the truth is that when I was at my all-time healthiest physically, I was in an all-out relational pit.

During that season I was eating so healthy that I refused to go to restaurants with my friends. I'd fix myself some chicken and sweet potatoes and steamed broccoli at home before meeting them to have fun. By the time I connected with them, I was always out of the loop. They'd been hanging out for a few hours by that point, and things just never clicked.

Similarly, when I was more structured with my weightlifting routines and goals, I neglected my time with God. I was so consumed with discipline in one area that it took priority over everything else. Instead of having fellowship with my best friends over a meal together, I'd be by myself in my apartment fixating on what to eat and how many calories to consume. Even though being healthy is a good thing, I took it to an unhealthy level to the detriment of more important things.

I've learned that the things that rule our lives affect our relationships.

I've always loved this exhortation from the apostle Paul to the believers in Corinth, which was to remember that once they said yes to Jesus, they said no to ruling their own lives. He told them that their bodies no longer belonged to them, that they now were *temples of God*. And the truth is that you and I can't "glorify God" in our bodies (v. 20) unless we're choosing to be healthy every day.

And by being "healthy," I don't mean obsessing over being in the gym to the point where you have no time for anything else or tightening your eating rules to the point where you can never enjoy a meal with your friends, family, or community. Being healthy doesn't mean being so overly rigid about getting your steps in that you walk right past the people you love.

On the flip side of that, sometimes we can neglect caring for our physical bodies. That's not good either because it's hard to love others well when we're tired, sluggish, and unfit. Being healthy is taking care of our bodies—our temples—so that we can do the will of God, serve each other, listen to each other, and love each other well.

Scripture is jam-packed with God's expectations for how His children are supposed to live, and all of those expectations require energy, attentiveness, and care. I know it's challenging to structure life according to God's priorities before we inject our own desires into the mix, but speaking from personal experience, life works a lot better that way.

HOW TO PUT LOVE FIRST

How are you doing with your temple? Do you need to slow down and make time for someone today, or do you need to turn your attention to your body and take a walk or cook a healthy meal at home? In the Huff home, we love trying new ways to make brussels sprouts taste amazing! A favorite of ours is to put them in the air fryer and drizzle hot honey on top. Today, take a walk with your family or a friend, or try a new healthy recipe and invite others to share it with you.

BE APPROACHABLE

Jesus said, "Let the little children come to me, and
do not hinder them, for the kingdom of heaven
belongs to such as these." MATTHEW 19:14 NIV

CHRISTIAN

A MAJOR REASON SADIE AND I DECIDED TO LIVE IN MONROE
after we got married was that so many of her family members live there
already, which meant there would be a built-in community for us. I
have to say, we absolutely made the right call. If we want a good time,
we just walk out the front door.

We spend a ton of time with Sadie's sister Bella and her husband,
Jacob, who is one of my closest friends. I love that I get to see him every
week—sometimes multiple times. He's a little wild and crazy like me,
and one thing I've noticed is that whenever our toddler nephews are
around, they make a beeline for Jacob and me. They know that we're
always up for a race to the trampoline and that, once we're there, we'll
throw them around like they're a couple of footballs. We'll return their
imaginary Spider-Man web with one of our own, and we'll keep it up
until they decide to switch to a pillow fight. They know that whenever
they come to us for fun, we'll never turn them away.

During Jesus' ministry here on earth, the Bible says that He went
about the countryside teaching people, healing people, and helping
people understand God. It was long and grueling work. It was worth-
while work, but it was difficult, and since Jesus was human just like
you and me, He needed a break from time to time. Every once in a
while in Scripture, we see glimpses of Jesus blowing off steam, kicking
back, and having a good time. In Matthew 19:13–15, for example,
Jesus had just finished a wearying stretch of ministry and was sitting

down to rest. Just then a bunch of adults brought children to Jesus, to see if He would lay hands on them and pray for them, which was a common way of bestowing blessings on someone in those days.

Well, the disciples who were with Jesus were upset by this. They knew that He needed some alone time, so they rebuked the people and told them to leave.

But Jesus had other ideas: "Let the little children come to me," He said, "and do not hinder them, for to such belongs the kingdom of heaven" (v. 14). What He was saying was that in the same way that children are drawn to people who will accept them and play with them and care for and love them, we're to come to Jesus just like that.

And it's a special thing to be that kind of person for the kids in your family or community as well.

> Every once in a while in Scripture, we see glimpses of Jesus blowing off steam, kicking back, and having a good time.

HOW TO PUT LOVE FIRST

If you have kids, you know that they are the most amazing and exhausting blessing you'll ever receive. Whether you are a parent or not, let's take today to love our communities by reaching out to a young family. Offer to babysit their children, drop off some food, or help with yardwork.

BE FUN-LOVING

A joyful heart is good medicine. PROVERBS 17:22

CHRISTIAN

THERE IS ABSOLUTELY A TIME AND PLACE FOR BEING serious—serious about my work, serious about my spiritual growth, serious about providing for my family, serious about praying for all the needs I see. But a day or week or month of all seriousness, and I'm no fun to be around. So Sadie and I take walks almost every evening. We play around with Honey and talk about our day. We laugh. We joke about cheesy shows on TV. We make funny faces at each other. Sound juvenile? It's not. It's part of what fills life with joy and fosters connection. It offers relief from hard times and refuels us to keep going.

Our birthdays happen to be days apart, so for the past several years we've made a point of throwing the most epic parties we can think of, inviting friends and family to be part of the fun. The year that I proposed to Sadie at one of those parties, the theme was the Olympics, and those who were there still talk about it today. We set up games all over the neighborhood where party guests had to accomplish different feats before they could move on. At one of those stations, they had to hit a golf ball over the pond—with a baseball bat. At another station, they had to serve a tennis ball over the net and into a taped-off square, using their nondominant hand. One station had a ping-pong challenge, another Spikeball. And every team had to balance a raw egg on a spoon in between all their feats.

It was amazing.

It was so ridiculously fun.

There were forty people at that party, and if you'd gone around and asked them about the tough stuff they were facing in life, you would have been sobered by the responses. Life is hard. But on that day, for those few hours, the tough stuff was pushed back for a minute. We were able to run and jump and laugh and do things we don't do in everyday life. And I like to think that when everyone reentered their "real" world the following day, they had a little spring in their step.

If you're the kind of person who is all about the fun and aren't worried about productivity because you're too busy living it up, then this exhortation isn't for you. But if you're the type who is super-productive, super-efficient, and super-hard on yourself whenever you take a break, then here goes: *lighten up*. Give yourself a minute to decompress. Shut your laptop and go have some fun tonight. I guarantee you won't regret it.

> If you're the type who is super-hard on yourself whenever you take a break, then here goes: *lighten up.*

HOW TO PUT **LOVE** FIRST

Do or plan something fun today. If you can't carve out time for today, plan it for the weekend. Give yourself a few hours to hang out with friends and family doing something that fills you with laughter. One thing we love to do is have themed car rides. Listen to ten minutes of rap, ten minutes of country, ten minutes of pop, or ten minutes of 2000s hits. It makes for a fun time.

BE REFLECTIVE

If we confess our sins, he is faithful and just to forgive us our
sins and to cleanse us from all unrighteousness. 1 JOHN 1:9

CHRISTIAN

I CAN'T REMEMBER WHAT SADIE AND I WERE TALKING
about, but based on what went down at the end of that conversation,
I'm guessing I was exasperated. Or maybe just hungry. Either way,
whatever showed up in my expression was something Sadie didn't like
at all.

"I wish you had a mirror right now," she said, "so you could see
how your face looks."

Those words sounded familiar to me.

In a flash I rewound to age twelve, when I'd get annoyed with
my brother or be rude to my mom, yet constantly denied it. My mom
would look at me and say, "I wish you had a mirror right now, so you
could see how your face looks."

"Did my mom tell you to say that to me?" I accused Sadie.
Laughing, she shook her head at me, asking me what in the world I
was talking about. "My mom. She used to *always* say that to me."

Sadie replied, "Well, now I can understand why."

According to both my mother and my wife, I evidently have a
tell when I've had enough during an interpersonal exchange. Or *three*
tells, to be more precise. I scoff—kind of a single-syllable laugh. I roll
my eyes. And I very subtly shake my head. They tell me I do all three
things simultaneously, which makes it pretty easy to tell when I'm
annoyed.

I know I do that stuff. I can feel my chest puff out. I can sense the
scoff coming up out of me. I can detect my eyes rolling way up toward

my brain. I know it's all happening as it happens; I just don't quite know how to make it stop. Or maybe it's that I'm just not *ready* to make it stop. Luke 6:45 tells us that our mouth speaks what our hearts are full of. And sometimes our faces show it too.

Even though I've made a lot of changes in my life since committing to following Jesus, there are still some patterns that are tough to change. I call those patterns "Old Christian," and I know they have to die. But some days, I'm just not ready yet. I'm not strong enough to let them go.

Maybe you can relate. Maybe you have a few patterns that you're still hanging on to, even though you know they don't square with God. My exasperation tell is pretty benign, but there are others I could share, deeper patterns that carry far worse consequences than irritating a parent or spouse.

As you learn more and more about Jesus, let His example be a mirror for you. From time to time, reflect on how well you're reflecting Him. And confess the ways you fall short.

Eventually, my prideful expression will change—and yours will too, I promise. It will change to look more like Christ. Our words, expressions, and hearts will overflow with Christ, and people will be drawn to Him through us.

HOW TO PUT LOVE FIRST

It's kind of amazing how important nonverbal communication is—and it's also kind of crazy how we can lack self-awareness in this area. Prayerfully observe yourself today: Are your expressions, tones, and body language reflecting Jesus? What might need to change?

BE PERSUADED

He said to all, "If anyone would come after me, let him deny
himself and take up his cross daily and follow me." LUKE 9:23

CHRISTIAN

AFTER DINNER ONE NIGHT SADIE WANTED TO GO TO DAIRY
Queen—which wouldn't have been a problem except that I wanted
Baskin-Robbins.

She had her work cut out for her that night. To say that I'm not
easily persuaded would be an understatement. You could call it stubborn, and you'd probably be right. Once I land on a conclusion, I don't
move off it quickly. It's not because I'm trying to be difficult; it's just
the way that I am wired.

So when Sadie wants DQ and I want Baskin-Robbins, what do I
do? I've had a lot of milkshakes in my life, and for me Baskin-Robbins
is always at the top—I won't be persuaded otherwise.

But I've noticed a funny thing happening the longer I walk with
Jesus Christ—it's getting increasingly tougher for me to stand firm in
my stubbornness. Yeah, I can talk the talk, but Jesus helps me walk
His walk. Whenever I'm in a situation where my stubborn pride wants
to reign, I stop and think about Jesus, about His complete willing-
ness to do whatever His Father wanted Him to do—every single time.
Something deep inside me shifts. I, too, want that level of obedience.
I want that level of compliance before God.

One time Jesus was teaching a small group of His disciples—His
closest friends—just after the feeding of the five thousand. They were
sitting there talking, when Jesus dropped a grenade in their laps.

He looked them in the eye and said, "If anyone would come after
me, let him deny himself and take up his cross daily and follow me. For

whoever would save his life will lose it, but whoever loses his life for my sake will save it. For what does it profit a man if he gains the whole world and loses or forfeits himself?" (Luke 9:23–25).

I know that in today's world people are all about living their best lives and being true to themselves and all that. But in this passage of Scripture, we see Jesus standing in opposition to that way of life. He doesn't want us to be persuaded by what the world says is okay to do or be; He wants us to be persuaded only by Him.

This approach doesn't come naturally to us. The last thing we want to do is give up our autonomy, our hard-won opinions, and hard-and-fast beliefs. But the calling on *all* of us who say we want to follow Jesus is to deny the things we're always so stubborn to cling to and to follow Him instead.

Will we let go of our preferences?

Will we let go of our desires?

Will we let go of how we've always done things?

Will we drop our will, our wants, our wishes, our ways, to live fully persuaded by Christ?

I want this kind of life, this kind of Spirit-reliant life, and I'm going to pursue it with all I've got. Even if it means radical change. Even if it means a complete reshaping. Even if it means—from time to time, anyway—DQ.

HOW TO PUT **LOVE** FIRST

Where do you struggle most with stubbornness or your own particular preferences? Work, family, church, your close relationships? What would it look like for you to release your grasp on a personal preference?

BE PRAYERFUL

He will cover you with his feathers. He will shelter
you with his wings. PSALM 91:4 NLT

SADIE

I WANT TO GIVE YOU AN IMAGE TO CARRY WITH YOU AS YOU work to care for the community God is giving you. It comes from Psalm 91, which starts like this: "Those who live in the shelter of the Most High will find rest in the shadow of the Almighty. This I declare about the LORD: He alone is my refuge, my place of safety; he is my God, and I trust him. . . . He will cover you with his feathers. He will shelter you with his wings" (vv. 1–2, 4 NLT).

This psalm took on new meaning for me during the months after Honey was born. I love to work—and to work hard. I love to dream big dreams and then try to execute them well, and I love to have a ton of activities on my calendar. But late last year my usually high energy level was no match for the challenges I faced. My ministry, Live Original, needed to hire new staff members. I had several relational situations that needed extra care. Christian and I were still relative newlyweds. And Honey—well, she was a newborn who needed her mama.

Over the years I had seen a counselor from time to time. In this season of overwhelming demands, I called her one day, saying, "Everyone needs me. There isn't enough of me to go around, and I feel like I'm letting everyone I care about down. Things are crazy-busy right now, and I need to be strong not just for myself, but for everyone else involved."

I don't remember her exact words to me that day, but the gist of what she said was this: "Sadie, only Jesus can carry the burdens you feel. You are not Jesus; He is."

It was one of those answers that is equal parts comforting and maddening. As she spoke, I sat there thinking, *Yeah, this all sounds totally right to me.* But the minute I got off the phone, I thought, *Wait, what am I supposed to do?*

Then the words of Psalm 91 popped to mind, and I couldn't help but smile as I pictured the size difference between God's wingspan and mine. I literally stretched out my arms as wide as they could reach and then had to laugh at myself. *Yeah, not very far, right, God?* I then pictured God, the Creator of the universe, His figurative wings spread wide. What *wasn't* covered by those wings? Nothing at all.

I love my husband, but guess who loves him more? *God does.* I cherish my little Honey girl, but guess who cherishes her more? *God does.* I love my team but—you guessed it—God loves them more. Whoever I care about, God cares about that person more. And He has committed Himself to protecting them, no matter what unfolds.

The best thing you can do for your people is to bring their burdens to the Lord and let God love them in the perfect way that only He can. You can show up, listen, and love, but God is the one who can heal and be all things for all people. Take the pressure off yourself and let God be God.

HOW TO PUT LOVE FIRST

Lay down your burdens today. Your close relationships, your work, or your ministry burdens. Whatever it is that has been hanging over you, write it down and surrender it to God. Pray and ask Him to carry your burdens for you. He will do it—He is able.

BE BOLD

For I am not ashamed of the gospel, for it is the power
of God for salvation to everyone who believes, to the
Jew first and also to the Greek. ROMANS 1:16

CHRISTIAN

WHEN I STARTED LIVING FOR GOD, SOME THINGS WERE
easier to change than others. It was easy to adjust daily rhythms and
make room for reading my Bible in the morning before class. It was
easy to pray in my truck when I was driving, rather than turning on
rap music.

But it *wasn't* so easy being the guy I was becoming in God around
my family.

A couple of years into my faith transformation, I met Sadie, and
she and I would talk on the phone for hours nearly every night about
the deepest things. It was easy for me to talk to her about the guy I
used to be versus the man I was becoming and share all my hopes about
what was to come as I surrendered more and more of myself to God.

But my parents and siblings—well, that was a different story.
It was like I was embarrassed about my relationship with Jesus, like
I was *ashamed* of who I now was because they had had a front-row
seat to who I was. It's not like my parents were anti-God; they were
Christians, but we hadn't openly talked about our testimonies. I didn't
know how to share with them how my life had been changed. And so,
for a while I just hid.

Flash forward to the week after Sadie and I got engaged and were
spending some time with my parents in Omaha. We were at a restaurant, and out of nowhere Sadie asked my mom and dad how they had
first come to know Jesus.

To say that things got awkward is an understatement. My parents froze, so Sadie looked at me and said, "Hey, why don't you start?"

Things got even more awkward then. I took a sip of my water and looked down at my hands. Sadie was sitting there so confused, probably thinking, *What's wrong? Aren't we all Christians here?*

After dinner, I walked Sadie to her room and said, "When we get back to Louisiana, I want to get baptized."

I'd never taken that step of obedience before but was ready to take it now. I was sick of playing both sides of the fence, on fire for Jesus in some settings and totally lukewarm in others.

And what was there to be ashamed of, anyway? Jesus had rescued me from utter darkness and had brought me into the light.

Was I really ashamed of that? It's unbelievable, as I look back.

Paul said, "For I am not ashamed of the gospel, for it is the power of God for salvation to everyone who believes" (Romans 1:16).

In Jesus there is no shame.

Three days later I got baptized and publicly identified myself with Jesus. He'd been my Savior; now He was my Lord.

I FaceTimed my parents afterward and was beaming and laughing and relieved. It was like something had broken off me that had been keeping me from owning up to my newfound faith. From there, the culture of our family shifted from that of keeping Jesus sidelined to putting Him in the very center of our lives. We started praying for each other. We started encouraging each other in our faith, something we'd never done before. And it all stemmed from Sadie's singular question: "How did you first come to know Jesus?"

HOW TO PUT LOVE FIRST

How did you first come to know Jesus? Write it down. Share it with your friends or family. That is no secret to keep—that is a powerful testimony! Boldly tell others about what Jesus has done for you.

BE A HELPER

Let us not become weary in doing good, for at the proper time we will reap a harvest if we do not give up. Therefore, as we have opportunity, let us do good to all people, especially to those who belong to the family of believers. GALATIANS 6:9–10 NIV

SADIE

I'LL NEVER FORGET THE DAY OF MY MOPED ACCIDENT. ONE minute, I was on vacation with a friend and her family in Florida, and the next, I was on the side of the road—alone, injured, and terrified.

Our group had gone out riding, and I was following behind my friend and her family, going a little too fast in order to keep up. It was definitely too fast for the day's conditions. It began to rain, and because I was behind everyone, none of them saw me lose control of my moped, which sent me straight to the side of the road and off the bike.

At forty-plus miles per hour, it really was a miracle I lived. By God's grace, I stood up and walked along the road looking for help. I was soaked from the rain and covered in blood as I approached a truck at a red light. A man opened his door, and all I could say was, "Sir, can you take me to the hospital?"

Without hesitation, he helped me into his truck and waited with me until the paramedics arrived. I have no idea where that man was supposed to be going or what plans he had to change to help me out. But in my desperate moment of need, he was there for me.

Showing up for God and our communities—even for strangers—is not always convenient. It often costs us something. Our time. Our money. A change in plans. I am sure I made that driver late to wherever he was going. But that afternoon, he stopped everything and took care of me.

In Mark 10, Jesus and His disciples were leaving Jericho when a blind beggar named Bartimaeus began calling for Him: "Jesus, Son of David, have mercy on me!" (v. 47).

Would you believe that many in the crowd tried to hush him and told him to be quiet? They wanted Jesus to ignore the man and keep going. I can't imagine if there had been someone else in the truck on the day of my accident telling the driver, "Don't stop for her. Keep going." Thankfully, that's not what happened to me or to Bartimaeus.

When Jesus heard Bartimaeus calling, He had great compassion and told the people to call him over.

"What do you want me to do for you?" Jesus asked him.

The blind man said, "Rabbi, I want to see."

"Go," said Jesus, "your faith has healed you." Immediately he received his sight and followed Jesus along the road. (vv. 51–52 NIV)

Jesus stopped that day. He delayed His journey. He paid attention to the man's needs. He was and is the ultimate Helper.

And He wants us to be like Him—eyes and ears open to those around us.

You might not find yourself at a dramatic scene like my moped accident, but people all around you need help. And what they need might not always be obvious. That is why it is so important we take the time to stop and ask, to really care for people.

HOW TO PUT LOVE FIRST

I understand how easy it is to get caught up in our own lives, families, and to-do lists. Sometimes it's like we have blinders on to everyone else's struggles. How can we take our blinders off today? Who can we help?

BE THOUGHTFUL

Therefore let us stop passing judgment on one another.
Instead, make up your mind not to put any stumbling block or
obstacle in the way of a brother or sister. ROMANS 14:13 NIV

SADIE

AFTER CHRISTIAN AND I DECIDED TO START PLANNING
events, inviting people over, and simply reaching out to others in our
community, our lives became filled with joy and fun. We started growing some amazing relationships and having experiences where people
who were once just acquaintances became dear and trusted friends—
people we do life with, people who help us know Jesus more and more.

But recently, at one of our get-togethers, a friend said something
along the lines of "This is so great. I remember thinking that you guys
probably wouldn't want to hang out because y'all are so busy."

Wait, what?

Why wouldn't we want to hang out with friends? If our lives were
so busy, wouldn't we especially need real friends to do normal things
with? At first, I was so confused. This person had come to some con-
clusions about Christian and me based on what he *thought* he knew
about us. But not based on *actually knowing* us and our needs.

But then . . . I was also convicted. I couldn't even get upset because
I realized how often I do the same thing. Don't we all?

For example, how often do we:

- Not invite or include someone because we think they're too
  busy and have better plans or other friends to hang out with?
- Not put ourselves out there with people because we're afraid
  they won't accept us or want to make time for us?

- Not speak up because we think we know what the other person is already thinking or how they will respond?

The list could go on and on with everything from us thinking we're better than others to being worried that we're not good enough for them. We often assume we know everything about a person or situation when, frankly, sometimes we're dead wrong.

Assumptions are an unnecessary barrier to connecting with people. They can be so subtle we don't even realize that we're making them or letting them control our decisions. And on the flip side, when we're the object of someone's assumptions, we can get defensive instead of introspective. We need to consider that perhaps there's some level of reality to what's being assumed based on something we've said or done in the past. But whether assumptions are wrong or painfully on point, thoughtful, open-hearted conversation can grow, restore, and repair relationships.

Rather than letting unspoken judgments and assumptions rule over us, we need to talk to each other, open our own lives, and walk with each other—it will be a better, more fulfilling way to live in community. I'm so glad that our friends didn't let initial assumptions keep them from getting to know us. We would have all missed out on so much.

HOW TO PUT LOVE FIRST

Let's spend some time thinking about assumptions that may be burdening us and holding us back from real connection. We've found it is always best to lay down any assumptions and invite people in. Even if they cannot come, that invitation speaks volumes—*you are wanted, you belong, you are a vital part of our lives.*

BE KIND

"Do not follow the crowd in doing wrong. When you
give testimony in a lawsuit, do not pervert justice
by siding with the crowd." EXODUS 23:2 NIV

SADIE

HAVE YOU EVER BEEN PART OF AN EXCITED CROWD?
Cheering for your team at a big game, worshiping God at an amazing
event, or singing at the top of your lungs at a concert? It's incredible
when people come together over something beautiful. However, it can
be disheartening and sometimes dangerous when people come together
over something they're not happy about.

When I was in middle school and high school, I loved playing
basketball. Loved it. By the time I was in high school, though, I wasn't
just known for loving basketball. I was known for my family and their
show, *Duck Dynasty*. And when the two of those things collided, it
was not a very fun experience. Like when the whole visiting crowd
would bring duck calls to the game to blow every time I dribbled or
shot the ball.

I'm not even kidding. I can laugh about it now, but as a teenage
girl, I found it less than hilarious. I often cried in the locker room after
the games because being singled out like that was hard and it truly
did mess with my game. Here I was trying to focus on my basketball
game to the sound of duck calls vibrating off the gymnasium walls,
mocking me.

There's a segment of psychology called crowd psychology or mob
psychology. It's the idea that a crowd of people can think and behave
in ways that are different from how the individuals in the crowd might
think or behave on their own. Let me give you an example: no one ever

walked up to me and blew a duck call in my face. Who would do that? But when surrounded by fifty of your closest friends and no one can single you out? Game on.

The Bible tells us that when Jesus journeyed back into Jerusalem at the triumphal entry, just days before the crucifixion, the crowds welcomed Him shouting, "Blessed is the King who comes in the name of the Lord! Peace in heaven and glory in the highest!" (Luke 19:38). People laid palm branches and their cloaks across the road as a colt carried Jesus into the city. This crowd hailed Him as a king.

Yet, only days later, Jesus was standing before Pilate in front of a crowd who was shouting, "Crucify him! Crucify him!" (Luke 23:21 NIV).

One Jesus. Two crowds. One group praising Him as king and promoting His glory, and one promoting His death.

It's important we pay attention to the "crowds" we're in, and it's important that we watch what triggers us and others. Whether it's booing at a game or jumping on social media commentary, we don't want to be part of the crowds that are ushering in hatred and death. We need to be intentional about where we are, who we are with, and how we use our voices. If you find yourself behaving or speaking in groups in ways you would never consider as an individual, it's time to stop.

Our world can be a hard place. Let's lock arms together to make it kinder and more loving, and to use our voices to promote God's glory.

HOW TO PUT **LOVE** FIRST

I mentioned social media as a place where the crowd can get rough. Today, make encouraging comments on a couple of your friends' posts, and say something nice on a celebrity's page! They might not respond, but that doesn't mean it wasn't reassuring to see.

BE A LEARNER

Likewise, you who are younger, be subject to the elders. Clothe yourselves, all of you, with humility toward one another, for "God opposes the proud but gives grace to the humble." 1 PETER 5:5

SADIE

A FEW WEEKS AGO AN AMAZING LEADER INTERVIEWED ME for his podcast, and during that conversation, I was struck by a couple of things. First off, I have admired this man's ministry for years and have listened to dozens of interviews where *he* was the one being interviewed. I've learned from him. I've been led by him. I've come to love Jesus more because of his influence in my life. And now this person was asking me the questions? He was seeking wisdom from *me*? It was a full-circle moment for sure. As he affirmed my leadership and the life I am living, I felt seen, supported, and esteemed.

Now to the two takeaways I made that day. Number one: for those of us who are "younger" (define that as you will!), the best possible posture we can assume in life is that of a persistent learner. Think of a sponge, ready to soak it all in. True, we can spend our time and energy elbowing past people and demanding that the world listen to what we have to say. But where does that leave us in the end? Embittered and isolated, actually, and having made very little impact at all. Far better to invest ourselves in learning all we can, so that when we open our mouths to speak, we have something wise to say.

> For those of us who are "younger," the best possible posture we can assume in life is that of a persistent learner.

So that's the first thing: *learn all we can.*

Here's the second thing: *let God lift us up.* The

very next verse in the 1 Peter 5 passage quoted above says this: "Humble yourselves, therefore, under the mighty hand of God so that at the proper time he may exalt you" (v. 6). In that little full-circle moment I described before, remember that I spent *years* learning from this world-class leader before I was called on to contribute my thoughts. And you know what? In God's view, it was right on time. I know it's tempting to want to promote ourselves, to prove ourselves, to show the world we're all that and more. But when we let God manage our elevation, when we let *God* decide to raise us up, we'll know that the opportunity is suitable for us, that in His strength we'll succeed at the task.

If you are in the workforce today, then this message is for you: invest yourself wholeheartedly in learning from those who are wiser than you, from those who have logged more time than you have. Be curious. Be humble. Show up every day ready to grow. Stay this course until *God* says you're ready to start sharing the things that you've learned.

HOW TO PUT LOVE FIRST

Just for today, ask more questions about what you *don't* know than you make declarations about what you do. And tomorrow? Do the same!

BE PEACEFUL

Let him seek peace and pursue it. 1 PETER 3:11

CHRISTIAN

EVER SINCE I MET SADIE, I HAVE BECOME A NIGHT OWL. IT all started when we would stay up hours past my normal time, talking on the phone about anything and everything we could think of. And still to this day, I go to bed late. If I had my way every day (and if Honey suddenly turned into a superstar sleeper), my head would hit my pillow around midnight, and I would get out of bed around nine. Suffice it to say, that's not exactly how things go. We have the first part down—most nights, we wind down by midnight—but here is the kicker: we are jolted awake around five in the morning by a very small girl experiencing very large hunger cravings.

That's true for a lot of us, right? We've got jobs, kids, commitments—something that's dictating our schedules. Here's what this means for me: If I'm not careful, I'll jump out of bed at a ridiculous hour to help Sadie get Honey settled and then try to sleep a little longer before actually getting up. At that point, I'll wake up and feel pressure to strive since the day seems to be getting away from me. I'll stress about the stuff I need to get done or the things I want to do, and before I know it, it will be midafternoon before I've focused a single thought on God.

I've found a better way: all throughout the day, I strive to spend time with Jesus, whether I'm sitting around the table with my family, driving my truck, lifting weights in the gym, or spending time

> If you long to bring peace with you as you walk through your day, then start that day with God.

with my friends. I've learned that when we prioritize our thoughts, actions typically follow from there.

If you long to bring peace with you as you walk through your day—going to work, running errands, hitting the gym, meeting a friend for lunch—then start that day with God. If you're the kind of person who sleeps with your phone six inches away (me too), then as soon as your eyes open, commit to reading a Bible app. If you sleep with your phone across the house and use a real alarm clock, then take a few minutes when you wake up to check in with God through prayer.

Try this approach for a week, and see if your relationships improve as a result. I know they will because God says it's so. When you seek peace, you will exude peace. You will bring peace wherever you go.

HOW TO PUT LOVE FIRST

When your eyes open tomorrow morning, before you do *anything else*, commit your heart—and your day—to the Lord. Ask Him to make you a person of peace.

BE TRUSTING

"Put out into the deep and let down your nets for a catch." LUKE 5:4

SADIE

CHRISTIAN AND I MET ON A BEACH AND STILL TODAY LOVE hanging out on a beach, so it's no surprise that some of our favorite stories from the Bible feature Jesus on a beach.

First, let me take you to a scene in Luke 5 where *insane* numbers of people were gathering to hear Jesus preach. So many people showed up that Jesus couldn't even be heard, which is why He climbed into Simon Peter's boat on the shore, turned to Simon Peter, and told him to put out a little from the land. He stood in the bottom of the fishing boat and preached to the crowds, and then as the people dispersed, He looked at Simon and said, "Put out into the deep and let down your nets for a catch" (v. 4).

Now, Simon had just heard Jesus preach and could probably tell there was something special about Him. But still, when Jesus told Simon to trust Him with a catch, Simon's response was to inform Jesus about the logistics: "Master," he said, "we toiled all night and took nothing!" But then Simon Peter said this: "But at your word I will let down the nets" (v. 5).

I *love* that line. That line represents humility. Obedience. Faithfulness even when Jesus' ask made no sense.

Not surprisingly, even after a fishless night for the men, verse 6 says that when Simon Peter and the others let down their nets, "they enclosed a large number of fish, and their nets were breaking."

The moral to this story? When Jesus is in your boat, everything changes.

I know celebrities who are famous for their award-winning work in film or music or sports, yet all they talk about when they're interviewed is how Jesus has changed their lives. They have Jesus in their boats.

I have tons of friends who use their social media platforms to talk about the goodness of God. Guess what's true of them? They have Jesus in their boats.

It's tempting to believe that the only place the good news of the gospel can get preached is in a church on a stage by a pastor who's formally ordained. But if Simon Peter were here, he'd tell a different story, a story of how Jesus approached him while he was minding his own business, just doing his job, and asked to get into his boat. He'd tell of how Jesus used that makeshift platform to bring people into a personal relationship with Him.

Jesus wants to be in your boat. Your boat is wherever you are. It is where you show up every day and spend time. It's your job. It's your school. It's your marriage. It's your family. It's your friendships. It's oftentimes the places we are so familiar with that we forget to invite the power of God in. But if we stop and think about it, it is in these spaces we need His power the most. These familiar places are the ones we have the most potential to impact.

Let Jesus into the places you think you know everything there is to know about because I promise He knows more.

HOW TO PUT **LOVE** FIRST

Think about the area in your life that you have been trying to thrive in without inviting Jesus into the picture. If it's your job, ask God what He can teach you within your position. If it is the major you are studying, ask God for wisdom in what you're learning and a purpose behind all the hard work.

BE LOVING

Beloved, let us love one another, for love is from God. 1 JOHN 4:7

CHRISTIAN

SADIE AND I LOVE EACH OTHER DEEPLY. MAYBE YOU'VE noticed that throughout this book. We love each other, and we love God. And to shoot straight, even though there are a lot of times when we don't fully understand what God is up to in our lives or in the world around us, we're not really the type of people who doubt Him. I mean, we *do* doubt Him from time to time. But usually it's fleeting. We don't make a pattern of doubting God. Or we hadn't, until we did.

For a long while every time Sadie took on a big ministry opportunity, something terrible went down in our family. With every yes we gave to serving God, it was like Satan himself hollered, "No!"

The final straw was when this seeming oppression started affecting our kid. We railed against God. And then, I'm sorry to say, we railed against each other. You know how sometimes you're so enraged by the way life is treating you that you don't know where to point all that energy? That was us. We decided to point it at each other, which is a strategy I don't recommend.

We made attempts to draw near to each other and to draw near to Jesus, but it wasn't working. We ended up in an all-out battle where we both unloaded all the accusations we'd been holding back.

It wasn't pretty.

I was scheduled to attend a men's retreat for three days, and while I wanted no part of it, given everything that was going on, Sadie encouraged me to go. I went. I sat there annoyed the entire first day. I would find myself rolling my eyes over how cheesy everything seemed. But by the second day in, I broke. I had *serious* walls up that weekend, and still, God made a way through. He, and the community of men around me, helped me get through my struggle.

Toward the end of the retreat, all fifty of us guys were given time and space to think about our relationship with God and to think about the important people in our lives. We could pray, journal, write a letter, whatever. I wrote a note to Sadie, and in it, I laid out my heart.

What I couldn't have known was that many of the things I wrote that day matched up exactly with the things Sadie had been praying over me while I'd been gone. Granted, we were only two miles apart while I was at the retreat, but emotionally, we were worlds away. And there in that quiet space, where for days on end I had no phone, no watch, and no sense of anything going on in the world outside that little campground, God met with me. He prompted me with specific words that my wife evidently needed to hear. He comforted me. He reassured me of His care for me. He filled me up, so I could have something to give. He loved me so I could love.

During the final hour of the retreat, friends and family gathered outside the meeting room to show their support for those of us who had been away. And when I saw Sadie there, her smile as wide as the sky, I couldn't help but grin and tear up. Later, she would read that letter and cry grateful tears. We would shake our heads over the goodness of God. She said to me she had never felt more loved by me and by God at the same time as she read those words.

I was back. She was back. We were us again. I'd let God in . . . I'd put Him first . . . and now love could have its way.

HOW TO PUT LOVE FIRST

You may not be tangled up in a relational knot today, but someday you'll find yourself there. My advice when you do is that you go get right with God. Let Him in—fully in. When He comes, love comes too.

PAUSE AND REFLECT WITH DR. JOSH KIRBY

HAVE YOU EVER BEEN A PART OF A TEAM IN SPORTS OR AT work where each team member's unique temperament and talent shine through as you work together toward a shared purpose? Perhaps you've had a coach or a team leader who truly valued each individual yet could also see the collective personality of the team and celebrate the beauty of coming together to create something even more dynamic.

God sees us in this way. He delights in us growing alongside others, building upon one another's strengths, and encouraging each other in our weaknesses. Whether we're cheering friends on in a church softball league, serving together in ministry, or sharing the ups and downs of our week in a small group, it is often through our shared lives in a community that He teaches us the most about our relationship with Him. Community is the added color to the canvas of our lives, through the people we live among. Their personalities, unique talents and gifts, and quirks help give life more meaning.

LEARNING IN LOVE

For all the added beauty of life in community, living purposefully in this way can be challenging at times. As we become more grounded in Christ, we will begin to mature and grow more secure in our closest relationships, but as we've learned, God does not limit his design for intimacy to only family and friends. We are also created with an intrinsic desire to connect, share life, and be of help in a community of people. He continues to deepen how we relate in love to everyone around us, from our classmates and coworkers to others we encounter who may be in the midst of grief, poverty, health crises, or other hard issues.

And though some of these interactions can be challenging relationally or stretch us out of our comfort zones, when we view our everyday interactions from the perspective of eternity, we take on a new mission in life. It is not our lot to just wait until Jesus returns, but to wake up each day with purpose, as someone who knows the hope for the world—that God is with us and will be always—and to share that with the people around us. God instilled this relational and spiritual nature within us so that through it, He can nurture, strengthen, and grow us through one another. For we are not meant to be alone.

> It is not our lot to just wait until Jesus returns, but to wake up each day with purpose.

HEALING IN LOVE

When I first meet with a new client in counseling, I always ask them to describe their social system. While I need to know about their family of origin and most important adult relationships before I step into the process of helping them, it is also valuable to understand their day-to-day personal interactions at work, in church, with acquaintances and friends, and anyone else that could have influence. Not only am I assessing how they prioritize their time and involvement in communal life, but I also want to know how they see my role of supporting them in the context of the support system they already may or may not have. This helps me have a sense of whether they will be willing to trust me.

Many people did not have an integrated sense of community when they were growing up and may struggle to find it as adults. Others who haven't been connected with other Christians in their lives may doubt that they are equipped well enough, they are "good enough," or they are relatable enough to help others as they meet people in their new life in Christ. And all of us have struggles and sins that we wish we could forget. For those who have experienced trauma in relationships,

> God's grace and mercy are sufficient for all of us, regardless of how we were raised or what we've been through.

what often leads to the ongoing effects of the harm is going through the trauma or the aftermath alone. This isolation in such pain can create strong feelings of distrust of others.

God's grace and mercy are sufficient for all of us, regardless of how we were raised or what we've been through. But trusting people to accept and help us—to be the hands and feet of Jesus—can sometimes be a difficult road for those of us who have little experience in a healthy community, are fearful of exposing our guilty pasts, or have been wounded by others—particularly by those who were meant to be trusted.

And yet, in spite of all of that, those who could hardly imagine opening up or trusting that a community of people would care enough to include them—much less value them for who they are—have found healing that transforms them into a new life because the sufficiency of God never fails, and His love never ends. The book of James in the Bible speaks of the healing power of sharing our stories and confessing our struggles within prayerful community. In our true conviction, when we confront sin, brokenness, isolation, and fear, the Holy Spirit's power in the safety of God's people is *mighty*. Carrying ourselves in a new light of a loving community changes our stories, changes us, and changes how we see God in our lives.

LEADING IN LOVE

Once we are secure, trusting in God's provision in the care of others in community, we see that we are also being called to leadership in His kingdom. We begin to find greater purpose in our lives and hear God calling us to lead right now, not in the far-off future. For some this involves influencing others through their careers, by directing ministries, or in their roles as teachers, mentors, or coaches. For others, it comes through service, hospitality, encouragement, and shared activities. Within a community of people, God instills each person with spiritual giftings accompanied by a unique purpose. The power of fellowship that comes from our purposed gifts working together is far stronger than anything we can do alone.

No matter how we are called to lead, we are to be intentional and authentic in God's will for us. To lead authentically in love, we must remain grounded in that which is greater than ourselves and our self-interests. For leaders in an organization, if they are focused more on making money than being good spouses or parents at home, that misalignment of values will eventually have a negative impact on the people they are leading, and ultimately themselves. Likewise, as Christians, if we are more focused on what we are getting from our communities rather than how God is using us through them, we will struggle to sustain our efforts. As you seek out or are invited to join in opportunities where you may lead and influence—whether socially, in service, or in ministering directly to others—spend a few moments allowing God to prepare your heart and mind to be used for His ultimate purpose.

> No matter how we are called to lead, we are to be intentional and authentic in God's will for us.

TRUTH IN LOVE

When I was training as an intern counselor and was beginning to work with couples, my supervisor at the time shared with me a very important piece of advice. He told me that I can't, whether pridefully or ignorantly, deny myself the same honesty with myself that I'm asking of my clients.

Counseling is relational, after all, and if I am unwilling to confront certain aspects of my life and relationships, then I will only be so valuable to my clients. While counselors don't regularly share the personal details of their own lives, people can sense if you are genuinely invested in what you are doing and certainly whether you can be authentically present with them in their concerns. Similarly, when we veil who we are in community, we can only go so far with others. When we find ourselves continuing to show up in community yet are only going through the motions, it is often a sign that we are trying to make up for our lack of connection in our own personal relationships with God or with close family and friends. Our cups are empty, but we still try to pour.

One way to reset as you prepare to step into other's lives in community is to take a regular inventory with God, prayerfully and truthfully acknowledging where you are in your sense of connection with trusted people and your almighty Father. In this communion with Him, ask for peace and strength to restore your heart and to repair what needs to be repaired in those relationships so that you are equipped to lead and love genuinely with a cup that runs over.

A LIGHT IN LOVE

In the Sermon on the Mount, Jesus declares us as the light of the world. This is not a call to be relevant or popular. Rather, it is a call to be useful in and reflective of God's presence on Earth as it is in heaven.

> As lights upon a stand, we are intended to illuminate God's work for others through us, not draw attention to ourselves.

In our often well-intentioned pursuits in our communities and social networks, we, of course, want to view our positions and platforms as honorable and helpful. Yet, when we focus on the platform more than the purpose, we are at risk of clouding others' views of God and shading our own. As lights upon a stand, we are intended to illuminate God's work for others through us, not draw attention to ourselves.

Shining as lights for the world, we are to remain patient, faithful, gentle, and self-controlled. The Spirit aids us, slowing us from pride, envy, anger, and insistence on our own motives. Paul proclaims in 1 Corinthians that a community of believers is made up of a diversity of originally designed and purposed people with unique gifts willed for God's common good. This reciprocal and connecting way of life not only strengthens us in our daily efforts, but continuously reveals to us the joy and presence of God. So, in your own community—your local church, your workplace, your neighborhood, your home—take joy that His presence has the power to bring people of any background together, reconcile any hurt, and through His people, create a spiritual community that spans time and history.

Shine a light on His relational kingdom, knowing that it can usher in healing, joy, and connection in your life and the lives of others, as we purposefully prepare for His return when we will enjoy His presence and the community of believers for eternity.

Angela Shoemaker, Unveiled Radiance Photography

ABOUT THE AUTHORS

SADIE ROBERTSON HUFF IS A *NEW YORK TIMES* BESTSELLING author, speaker, influencer, and founder of Live Original. Communicating as a sister and friend, Sadie is on a mission to reach the world with the message of Christ. The host of the popular podcast *Whoa, That's Good*, which launched in 2018, she continues to top charts and minister to millions of listeners as she engages with current leaders, asking them to answer one question: "What is the best advice you have ever been given?" *Live Original*, Sadie's blog, features encouraging and transparent messages from her and her closest friends, and she is also founder of the online community and app *LO Sister*, which are designed to cultivate sisterhood through Bible studies and workshops. She also hosts the LO Sister conference annually in her hometown, Monroe, Louisiana.

CHRISTIAN HUFF IS A GRADUATE OF AUBURN UNIVERSITY. HE married Sadie Robertson in November 2019. Christian is the host of the *4:8 Men* podcast, which encourages men to train physically and spiritually, and averages more than 50,000 downloads per month. He is on a mission to see lives changed by the gospel of Jesus. He and Sadie Robertson Huff reside in Louisiana with their daughters and dog, Cabo.

DR. JOSH KIRBY IS A LICENSED PSYCHOLOGIST AND PARTNER at Sparrow House Counseling in Texas. He holds master's and doctoral degrees in Psychology as well as an MBA. He is an experienced counselor and presenter, specializing in marriage and relationship dynamics, emotional and spiritual health, and is a sought-after resource for leaders and high performers. He and his family live in Dallas.

Do you want to be noticed?
Or do you want to be *known*?

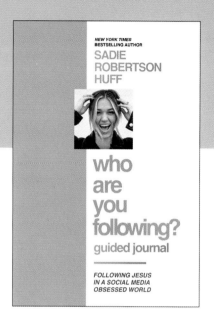

In *Who Are You Following?*—and its interactive companion, *Who Are You Following? Guided Journal*, designed to enrich your study experience— Sadie shares her story of finding offline joy, guides us in taking control of social media in our lives, and helps us see what the Bible has to do with any of it. Get ready to explore how to:

- become healthier by choosing who you follow on social media
- be thoughtful about who and what you pursue online
- escape the damaging mindset of comparison and feeling *not enough*
- let go of always making yourself look like you have it all together and, instead, to rest in God's love for you
- get the *best* out of your relationship with social media and be the light in the world

Live

WHO GOD CREATED YOU TO BE

Whether you have a long-time relationship with God or are new to faith, Sadie encourages young readers to make the most of each moment, make wise decisions, and always seek the truth of God's Word.

AVAILABLE WHERE BOOKS ARE SOLD